#30309

S0-FQL-590

DISCARDED

DISCOVERING CAREERS FOR YOUR FUTURE

nature

Coopersville Junior High
Media Center

Ferguson Publishing Company
Chicago, Illinois

Carol Yehling
Editor

Beth Adler, Herman Adler Design Group
Cover design

Carol Yehling
Interior design

Bonnie Needham
Proofreader

Library of Congress Cataloging-in-Publication Data

Discovering careers for your future. Nature.
     p. cm.
  Includes index.
  ISBN 0-89434-396-3
1.Natural history—Vocational guidance—Juvenile literature. 2.Nature conservation—Vocational guidance—Juvenile literature. [1. Natural history—Vocational guidance. 2. Nature conservation—Vocational guidance.] I.Title: Nature. II. Ferguson Publishing Company.

QH49 .D57 2001
508'.023—dc21

2001033026

Published and distributed by
Ferguson Publishing Company
200 West Jackson Boulevard, 7th Floor
Chicago, Illinois 60606
800-306-9941
www.fergpubco.com

Copyright © 2002 Ferguson Publishing Company
ISBN 0-89434-396-3

All Rights Reserved. This book may not be duplicated in any way without the express permission of the publisher, except in the form of brief excerpts or quotations for the purposes of review. The information contained herein is for the personal use of the reader and may not be incorporated in any commercial programs, other books, databases or any kind of software without written consent of the publisher. Making copies of this book or any portion for any purpose other than your own is a violation of United States copyright laws.

Printed in the United States of America
Y-9

Table of Contents

Introduction 1
Adventure Travel Specialists 6
Biologists 10
Botanists 14
Ecologists 18
Environmental Engineers 22
Fish and Game Wardens 26
Foresters 30
Geologists 34
Hazardous Waste Management Technicians 38
Land Trust or Preserve Managers 42
Naturalists 46
Oceanographers 50
Park Rangers 54
Pollution Control Technicians 58
Range Managers 62
Soil Conservation Technicians 66
Soil Scientists 70
Tree Experts 74
Wildlife Photographers 78
Zoologists 82
Glossary 86
Index of Job Titles 90
Nature on the Web 92

Introduction

You may not have decided yet what you want to be in the future. And you don't have to decide right away. You do know that right now you are interested in nature. Do any of the statements below describe you? If so, you may want to begin thinking about what a career in nature or the environment might mean for you.

___Science is my favorite subject in school.
___I am concerned about endangered species.
___I enjoy being outdoors.
___I am interested in wild animals.
___I am active in recycling projects.
___I like to study the plants and trees native to my area.
___I spend a lot of time hiking in the woods or through parks.
___I worry about air, water, and soil pollution.
___I participate in community clean-up projects.
___I would rather live in the country than in a city.
___My main hobby is gardening.
___It upsets me to hear about events like oil spills and rainforest destruction.
___I am interested in farming and agriculture.

Discovering Careers for Your Future: Nature is a book about careers in nature, from adventure travel specialists to zoologists. Nature careers involve working with wild animals, plants and trees, soil and land, and water. Some nature careers, such as biology, botany, geology, and zoology careers, focus on studying and learning more about the natural world. Others, such as ecology, pollution control, land preservation, and forestry careers, work at conserving and protecting the world. People in nature-related careers are interested in and deeply concerned about how humans interact with and change our planet.

This book describes many possibilities for future careers in nature. Read through it and see how the different careers are connected. For example, if you are interested in animal life, you will want to read the chapters on Biologists, Fish and Game Wardens, Naturalists, Oceanographers, Park Rangers, Wildlife Photographers, and Zoologists. If you are interested in ecology, you will want to read the chapters on Ecologists, Environmental Engineers, Foresters, Land Trust or Preserve Managers, Pollution Control Technicians, and Soil Conservation Technicians. Go ahead and explore!

What do nature workers do?

The first section of each chapter begins with a heading such as "What Botanists Do" or "What Range Managers Do." It tells what it's like to work at this job. It describes typical responsibilities and assignments. You will find out about working conditions. Which workers spend most of their time outdoors in undeveloped areas? Which ones work in laboratories or offices? This section answers all these questions.

How do I get into a nature career?

The section called "Education and Training" tells you what schooling you need for employment in each job—a high school diploma, training at a junior college, a college degree, or more. It also talks about on-the-job training that you could expect to receive after you're hired, and whether or not you must complete an apprenticeship program.

How much do people in nature careers earn?

The "Earnings" section gives the average salary figures for the job described in the chapter. These figures give you a general idea of how much money people with this job can make. Keep in mind that many people really earn more or less than the amounts given here because actual salaries depend on many different things, such as the size of the company, the location of the company, and the amount of education, training, and experience you have. Generally, but not always, bigger companies located in major cities pay more than smaller ones in smaller cities and towns, and people with more education, training, and experience earn more. Also remember that these figures are current averages. They will probably be different by the time you are ready to enter the workforce.

What will the future be like for nature careers?

The "Outlook" section discusses the employment outlook for the career: whether the total number of people employed in this career will increase or decrease in the coming years and whether jobs in this field will be easy or hard to find. These predictions are based on economic conditions, the size and makeup of the population, foreign competition, and new technology. Terms such as "faster than the average," "about as fast as the average," and "slower than the average," are terms used by the U.S. Department of Labor to describe job growth predicted by government data.

Keep in mind that these predictions are general statements. No one knows for sure what the future will be like. Also remember that the employment outlook is a general statement about an industry and does not necessarily apply to everyone. A determined and talented person may be able to find a job in an industry or career with the worst kind of outlook. And a person without ambition and the proper training will find it difficult to find a job in even a booming industry or career field.

Where can I find more information?

Each chapter includes a sidebar called "For More Info." It lists organizations that you can contact to find out more about the field and careers in the field. You will find names, addresses, phone numbers, and Web sites.

Extras

Every chapter has a few extras. There are photos that show nature workers in action. There are sidebars and notes on ways to explore the field, related jobs, fun facts, profiles of people in the field, or lists of Web sites and books that might be helpful. At the end of the book you will find a glossary and an index. The glossary gives brief definitions of words that relate to education, career training, or employment that you may be unfamiliar with.

The index includes all the job titles mentioned in the book. It is followed by a list of general nature Web sites.

It's not too soon to think about your future. We hope you discover several possible career choices. Happy hunting!

Adventure Travel Specialists

Americans Love Adventure

According to the Travel Industry Association of America, one-half of U.S. adults, or 98 million people, have taken an adventure trip in the past five years. Thirty-one million adults participated in hard adventure activities like whitewater rafting, scuba diving and mountain biking.

The World Tourism Organization reports that in 1997 there were more than 595 million international travelers, 40 to 60 percent of whom were nature tourists and 20 to 40 percent were wildlife tourists.

What Adventure Travel Specialists Do

Adventure travel specialists plan, and sometimes lead, tours of unusual, exotic, remote, or wilderness places. Most adventure travel involves some physical activity that takes place outdoors. There are two kinds of adventure travel—hard and soft adventure. *Hard adventure* involves high physical activity and advanced skill. Some examples of hard adventure are mountain biking, white water rafting, or rock climbing. *Soft adventure,* such as hot air ballooning, horseback riding trips, or bird-watching, is less physical and more family-oriented.

A popular type of adventure travel is the ecotour. This kind of trip combines the exciting thrill of adventure with travel to natural areas that conserve the environment and respect the well-being of the local people. A tour of the Asian rainforests, a trek to the Amazon jungle, or a trip to the Galapagos Islands are some examples of ecotours.

Some adventure travel specialists work in offices planning trips. They make transportation arrangements, order supplies, arrange lodging, and all other details for a successful vacation. They also promote and sell tour packages. Specialists that lead the tours are called *outfitters*. Some adventure specialists do both planning and leading of tours.

Outfitters and *guides* demonstrate any activities involved on the trip, help with the equipment, or help any group member having difficulties. They also speak about the location, scenery, history, wildlife, and unusual aspects of the region where the group is traveling. Guides help tour members in emergency situations, or during unplanned events. They are prepared to handle injuries, dangerous areas, and crisis situations.

Education and Training

High school classes such as geography, social studies, and history will prepare you for work as an adventure travel specialist. Speech or English classes will improve your public speaking skills. If you specialize in ecotravel, then study

EXPLORING

• Explore hobbies, such as scuba diving, sailing, hiking, mountain biking, canoeing, or fishing. Check your local phone directory for clubs and organizations that focus on these specialties.

•Read magazines, such as these:
Outside
http://www.outsidemag.com
Backpacker
http://www.backpacker.com
Bicycling
http://www.bicycling.com

• Research environmental groups, such as these:

National Audubon Society
1901 Pennsylvania Avenue, NW, Suite 1100
Washington, DC 20006
http://www.audubon.org

National Wildlife Federation
8925 Leesburg Pike
Vienna, VA 22184
http://www.nwf.org

Sierra Club
85 Second Street
2nd Floor
San Francisco, CA 94105-3441
http://www.sierraclub.org

WHAT IS AN ECOTOURIST?

An ecotourist's idea of a perfect vacation is not sitting by the pool sipping lemonade. According to the Ecotourism Society, ecotourists look for "responsible travel to natural areas that conserves the environment and sustains the well-being of local people." Here's a profile of the average Eco-Joe:

- Average age is between 35 and 54 years old.
- Even percentages of men and women enjoy ecotravel.
- 82 percent are college graduates.
- 60 percent prefer to travel as a couple, 15 percent with families, and 13 percent alone.
- Ecotourists prefer long trips—8 to 14 days.
- They don't pinch pennies—26 percent are willing to spend $1,000 to $1,500 per trip.
- The top three tours of choice are:
    1. wilderness setting
    2. wildlife viewing
    3. hiking or trekking

subjects such as earth science, biology, geology, and anthropology. A college degree is not required, but many companies prefer to hire those who have earned one, especially a degree in health, physical education, or recreation. If you plan to manage your own travel business someday, you should take a class in business administration, either at a university or a trade school.

Your experience and skill in a physical activity is important in this career. Take classes or join clubs in your area of interest, such as rock climbing, ballooning, or photographing wildlife.

Certain activities, such as scuba diving, may require formal training and a license examination. All travel guides should have training in emergency first aid and CPR.

Earnings

According to a Canadian university that offers two-year programs in adventure travel, graduates can make between $125 and $225 per day, or $17,000 for a three- to four-month season. Experienced guides with some managerial responsibilities can earn up to $65,000 a year. Tour leaders receive free food and accommodations, as well as a daily allowance while conducting a tour.

Outlook

There is a growing demand for adventure travel. This is because more people are interested in the environment and conservation, as well as physical fitness. There is a lot of competition for adventure travel jobs. Hundreds of people may apply for a single job. Those with experience in adventure travel or a unique specialty will have the best chances for employment. The U.S. Department of Labor says employment of travel agents should grow about as fast as the average through 2008.

FOR MORE INFO

The Adventure Travel Society
228 North F Street
Salida, CO 81201
719-530-0171
http://www.adventuretravel.com

For information on the ecotourism industry and related careers, contact:
The Ecotourism Society
PO Box 755
North Bennington, VT 05257
802-447-2121
http://www.ecotourism.org

For a listing of tour operators by state, and information on education and scholarships, contact:
National Tourism Foundation
546 E. Main Street
PO Box 3071
Lexington, KY 40596-3071
800-682-8886
http://www.ntaonline.com

Biologists

Activities for Budding Biologists

If you have one of these hobbies, you may have a future as a biologist:

Birdwatching

Collecting butterflies and other insects

Gardening

Microscope study

Raising or caring for animals

Watching nature shows

Visiting nature preserves

Going to the zoo

What Biologists Do

Biologists study how plants and animals grow and reproduce. Sometimes called *biological scientists* or *life scientists,* they often have other job titles because they specialize in one area of biology. *Botanists,* for example, study different types of plants. *Zoologists* study different types of animals. Biologists study living things, while chemists, physicists, and geologists study nonliving matter like rocks and chemicals.

Biologists may do their research in the field or in the laboratory. Their exact job responsibilities vary depending on their area of interest. For example, *aquatic biologists* study plants and animals that live in water. They may do much of their research on a boat studying the water temperature, amount of light, salt levels, and other environmental conditions in the ocean. They then observe how fish and other plants and animals react to these environments.

A biologist examines a specimen under a microscope.

No matter what type of research biologists do, they must keep careful records to note all procedures and results. Because biologists may sometimes work with dangerous chemicals and other materials, they always must take safety precautions and carefully follow each step in an experiment.

Some biologists advise businesses and governmental agencies. Others inspect foods and other products. Many biologists write articles for scientific journals. Some may also teach at schools or universities.

Education and Training

If you are thinking about a career in biology, you should plan to take high school

EXPLORING
- You can learn about the work of biologists at school field trips to federal or private laboratories and research centers.
- Visit your local museums of natural history or science, aquariums, and zoos.
- Many park districts offer classes and field trips to help you explore plant and animal life.

What Do Microbiologists Do?

Microbiologists are scientists who study bacteria, viruses, molds, algae, yeasts, and other organisms of microscopic size. They study the form and structure of these microorganisms, how they reproduce, and how they affect other living things, such as humans, animals, and plants. Microbiologists work in laboratories at universities, research facilities, and medical institutions, such as hospitals.

Medical microbiologists diagnose, treat, and prevent disease. They use blood and tissue samples from patients and try to find the microbes that cause illness, called pathogens. Clinical microbiologists also try to diagnose and prevent disease. Microbiologists' research has helped to prevent the spread of many diseases, including typhoid fever, influenza, measles, polio, whooping cough, and smallpox. Today, microbiologists are trying to find cures for such diseases as AIDS, cancer, cystic fibrosis, and Alzheimer's disease.

Many microbiologists work in the food industry. They identify pathogens in restaurant kitchens or in processed food that cause salmonella food poisoning. Microbiologists have identified many microorganisms useful to humans. Such microorganisms have been used in the making of food, such as cheese, bread, and tofu. Others are used to preserve food and tenderize meat. Flavors, colors, and added vitamins are all made from microbes.

Microbiologists also work in industry. They make sure manufactured goods are safe. In the pharmaceutical industry, they develop new drugs, such as antibiotics. Microbiologists also test new drugs and cosmetics. They develop new products, such as biological washing detergents. Some microbiologists work for water companies or environmental agencies. They test the quality of water.

courses in biology, chemistry, mathematics, physics, and a foreign language. After high school, you must go to college, where you will take more advanced courses in biology, math, chemistry, and physics. Then you choose a specialty. Specialties include microbiology, bacteriology, botany, ecology, or anatomy. Most successful biologists also have a master's degree or a doctorate in biology or a related field.

Earnings

The average salary for a biologist ranges from $28,000 to more than $86,000 a year. The median salary is $46,000. Government biologists with bachelor's degrees earn salaries of about $56,600 a year. Microbiologists who work for the federal government earn about $62,600.

Outlook

The U.S. Department of Labor predicts that employment of biologists will grow faster than average through 2008. There is a large number of people in this profession, so those with the most education and training will get the best jobs. Discoveries in genetics, leading to new drugs, improved crops, and medical treatments should open new job opportunities.

> ### FOR MORE INFO
>
> *For information about a career as a biologist, contact:*
> **American Institute of Biological Sciences**
> 1444 I Street, NW, Suite 200
> Washington, DC 20005
> http://www.aibs.org
>
> *For a career brochure and career-related articles, contact:*
> **American Physiological Society**
> Education Office
> 9650 Rockville Pike
> Bethesda, MD 20814-3991
> http://www.faseb.org/aps
>
> *For information on careers and educational resources, contact:*
> **American Society for Microbiology**
> Office of Education and Training—Career Information
> 1752 N Street, NW
> Washington, DC 20036
> http://www.asmusa.org

Botanists

It's a Bug's Life

Though many bugs are harmful to plants, some can be beneficial. These bugs prey on plant-feeding insects, and it isn't pretty—the following scenes of violence may not be suitable for all readers!
LADYBUGS eat aphids, mealy bugs, and mites. Adults may eat 50 or more aphids a day.
PRAYING MANTIS kill their plant-feeding prey by biting the back of the neck, severing the main nerves.
LACEWINGS suck the body fluids from their prey and carry the remains of their victims on their backs.
HOVER FLIES grasp plant-feeding insects and puncture them using tiny hooks in their mouths.

What Botanists Do

Botanists study plants, including cell structure; how plants reproduce; how plants are distributed on Earth; how rainfall, climate, and other conditions affect them; and more.

Botany is a major branch of biology. Botanists play an important part in modern science and industry. Their work affects agriculture, agronomy (soil and crop science), conservation, forestry, and horticulture. Botanists develop new drugs to treat disease. They find more food resources for developing countries. They discover solutions to environmental problems.

Botanists who specialize in agriculture or agronomy try to develop new varieties of crops that better resist disease. Or they may try to improve the growth of crops such as high-yield corn. These botanists focus on a specific type of plant species, such as ferns (pteridology), or plants that are native to a specific area, such as wet-

A Forest Service botanist takes a close look at one of the plants in the Sand Dunes area of the Hiawatha National Forest in Michigan.

land or desert. Botanists who work in private industry, such as a food or drug company, may focus on developing new products, or they may test and inspect products.

Research botanists work at research stations at colleges and universities and botanical gardens. Botanists who work in conservation or ecology often do their work out in the field. They help recreate lost or damaged ecosystems, direct pollution cleanups, and take inventories of species.

There are many specialties in botany. *Ethnobotanists* study how plants are used by a particular culture or ethnic group to treat diseases and injuries. *Ecologists*

Exploring

- Take part in science fairs and clubs.
- Volunteer to work for parks, nurseries, farms, labs, camps, florists, or landscape architects.
- Tour a botanical garden in your area and talk to staff.
- Grow your own garden, including fruits and vegetables, herbs, flowers, and indoor plants. Keep a notebook to record how each plant responds to watering, fertilizing, and sunlight.
- Hobbies like camping, photography, and computers are useful, too.

study the connection between plants and animals and the physical environment. They restore native species to areas, repair damaged ecosystems, and work on pollution problems. *Forest ecologists* focus on forest species and their habitats, such as forest wetlands. *Mycologists* study fungi and apply their findings to medicine, agriculture, and industry. *Plant cytologists* use powerful microscopes to study plant tissues in order to discover why some cells become malignant and cause the plant to get sick or die. *Plant geneticists* study the origin and development of inherited traits, such as size and color.

What Do Horticulturalists Do?

Horticultural technicians grow and sell plants and flowers that make our surroundings more beautiful. They work with flowers, shrubs, trees, and grass. Horticultural technicians plant and care for grass and trees in parks, on playgrounds, and along public highways. There are nearly 1 million people employed in landscape and horticultural services.

Horticultural technicians usually specialize in one of the following areas: floriculture (flowers), nursery operation (shrubs, hedges, and trees), turfgrass (grass), and arboriculture (trees).

Technicians plant seeds; transplant seedlings; inspect crops for nutrient deficiencies, insects, diseases, and unwanted plant growth; remove substandard plants; and prune other plants. Horticultural technicians feed nutrients to plants and flowers. They regulate humidity, ventilation, and carbon dioxide conditions. They use herbicides, fungicides, and pesticides to protect plants.

Related Jobs

Biologists
Ecologists
Foresters
Naturalists

Education and Training

If you want to become a botanist, you will have to go to college and earn a bachelor's degree. For research and teaching positions, you will have to study even longer, and go on to earn a master's or even a doctoral degree. These higher degrees require you to specialize in one of the many areas of botany mentioned in the section, What Botanists Do. For example, a master's in conservation biology focuses on the conservation of specific plant and animal communities.

Earnings

The National Association of Colleges and Employers reports that in 1999 botanists with a bachelor's degree earned an average of $29,000 to start. Those with a master's degree earned $34,450 and those with a Ph.D. earned $45,700. According to the U.S. Department of Labor, the top 10 percent of botanists earned $86,000 a year.

For More Info

Contact the following organization for a free booklet on careers in botany:
Botanical Society of America
Business Office
1735 Neil Avenue
Columbus, OH 43210-1293
614-292-3519

Contact this group about volunteer positions in natural resource management:
Student Conservation Association
PO Box 550
Charlestown, NH 03603
603-543-1700
http://www.sca-inc.org

Outlook

Employment for botanists is expected to increase faster than the average in the next decade. Botanists will be needed to help with environmental, conservation, and pharmaceutical issues. Botanists work in such a wide variety of fields that some type of employment is almost guaranteed.

Ecologists

Words to Learn

Canopy: The upper layer of a forest, created by the foliage and branches of the tallest trees.
Coniferous: Trees that bear cones.
Ecosystem: A community of animals and plants and their interaction with the nonliving environment.
Effluent: Wastewater or sewage that flows into a river, lake, or ocean.
Riparian zone: Forest or grass growing on the banks of a stream. The riparian zone can prevent soil erosion.
Savanna: A flat, grassy plain found in tropical areas.
Tundra: A cold region where the soil under the surface of the ground is permanently frozen.
Watershed: The gathering ground of a river system, a ridge that separates two river basins, or an area of land that slopes into a river or lake.

What Ecologists Do

Ecologists study how plants and animals interact and sustain each other in their environments. An environment not only includes living things, but also nonliving elements, such as chemicals, moisture, soil, light, temperature, and manmade things, such as buildings, highways, machines, fertilizers, and medicines. The word ecology is sometimes used to describe the balance of nature.

Much of ecologists' work involves the study of communities. A *community* is the group of organisms that share a particular habitat, or environment. For example, a *forest ecologist* might research how changes in the environment affect forests. They may study what causes a certain type of tree to grow abundantly, including light and soil requirements, and resistance to insects and disease.

Some ecologists study *biomes,* which are large communities. Examples of biomes are the tropical rain forest, the prairie, the tundra, and the desert. The ocean is sometimes considered as one biome.

Many ecologists focus their studies on the *ecosystem*—a community together with its nonliving components. *Population ecologists* study why a certain population of living things increases, decreases, or remains stable.

Since all living things, including humans, are dependent on their environments, the work of ecologists is extremely important in helping us understand how it works. An example of how the study of ecology help us is farming. Ecologists help farmers grow crops in the right soils and climates, provide livestock with suitable food and shelter, and eliminate harmful pests.

The study of ecology helps protect, clean, improve, and preserve our environment. Ecologists investigate industry and government actions and help correct past environmental problems.

Education and Training

To be an ecologist you must go to college and earn a bachelor of science degree. Recommended majors are biology,

EXPLORING

• Join a scouting organization or environmental protection group to gain firsthand experience in the work of an ecologist.

• Visit natural history museums. Visit nearby parks or forest preserves. What kinds of trees and plants grow there? Which insects, animals, and birds are native to the area?

• You will find lots of reading material at your library or bookstore. Here are a couple of suggestions:

The Amazon: Past, Present and Future by Alain Gheerbrant (Harry N. Abrams, 1992).

The Deserts of the Southwest by Maria Mudd Ruth (Marshall Cavendish Corp., 1998).

botany, zoology, chemistry, physics, or geology.

You will need a master's degree for research or management jobs. For higher positions, such as college teacher or research supervisor, you need a doctoral degree.

You must be able to work on your own or as part of a team. You must have good writing skills, which are important for writing reports.

ECOLOGICAL CATASTROPHE

Humans sometimes try to improve the environment and end up making big mistakes because they don't understand ecological balance. An example of an ecological catastrophe occurred in Borneo shortly after World War II. A program was undertaken there to control mosquitoes by spraying DDT. The number of mosquitoes declined drastically, but the roofs of houses began to collapse because they were being eaten by caterpillars. The caterpillars had previously been held under control by certain predatory wasps—which had been killed off by the DDT.

In addition to spraying for mosquitoes, the villagers also sprayed inside their homes to kill flies. Previously, the houseflies had been more or less controlled by lizards called geckos. As the geckos continued eating houseflies, now laden with DDT, the geckos began to die. The dead or dying geckos were eaten by house cats. The cats also began to die from the DDT concentrated in the bodies of the geckos they were eating. So many cats died that rats began invading the houses, eating the villagers' food. The rats multiplied and eventually became potential plague carriers.

The Evolution of Ecology

The term "ecology" was first defined in 1866 by Ernst von Haeckel (1834-1919), a German biologist. He grappled with Charles Darwin's (1809-82) theory of evolution based on natural selection. This theory said that those species of plants and animals that were best adapted to their environment would survive. Haeckel did not agree with Darwin, but he and many other scientists grew fascinated with the links between living things and their physical environment. Recognizing that there was such a link was a key step in the development of the science of ecology.

Physical strength is necessary for some field work.

Earnings

The average salary for ecologists is about $45,000 a year. With experience and a Ph.D., you can earn $85,000 or more. Most private companies pay higher salaries than the federal government.

Outlook

The job outlook for environmental workers in general should remain strong in the next decade. But there will be fewer jobs in land and water conservation. This is because so many ecologists compete for these popular jobs. Also, many environmental organizations have tight budgets.

The word ecology comes from the Greek words oikos (place we live) and logos (study of).

FOR MORE INFO

For more information about a career as an ecologist, contact the following organizations:
American Geological Institute
4220 King Street
Alexandria, VA 22302-1502
703-379-2480
agi@agiweb.org
http://www.agiweb.org

Ecological Society of America
2010 Massachusetts Avenue, NW
Suite 420
Washington, DC 20036-1023
202-833-8773
esahq@esa.org
http://www.sdsc.edu/projects/ESA/esa.htm

For information on student volunteer activities, contact:
Student Conservation Association
689 River Road
PO Box 550
Charlestown, NH 03603-0550
603-543-1700
http://www.sca-inc.org

For information on careers, publications, and internships, contact:
Environmental Careers Organization
National Office
179 South Street
Boston, MA 02111
617-426-4375
http://www.eco.org

Environmental Engineers

Silent Spring Speaks Loud and Clear

The publishing of Rachel Carson's book, *Silent Spring*, in 1962 marked the beginning of the environmental movement. The well-researched book drew the public's attention to the widespread use of pesticides and their effect on the world. The title refers to Carson's belief that fewer species of birds would be singing each spring unless pesticide poisoning was stopped. Readers suddenly became aware of the amount of air, water, and soil pollution that was threatening plant, animal, and human life. The environmental movement grew and spread throughout the 1960s. In 1970, governmental officials set up the Environmental Protection Agency, to enforce environmental protection standards, provide assistance to others combatting pollution, and develop and recommend new policies for environmental protection.

What Environmental Engineers Do

If a private company or a municipality does not handle its waste streams properly, it can face thousands or even millions of dollars in fines for breaking the law. A waste stream can be anything from wastewater, to solid waste (garbage), to hazardous waste (such as radioactive waste), to air pollution. *Environmental engineers* play an important role in controlling waste streams.

Environmental engineers may plan a sewage system, design a manufacturing plant's emissions system, or develop a plan for a landfill site needed to bury garbage. Scientists help decide how to break down the waste, but engineers figure out how the system will work. They decide where the pipes will go, how the waste will flow through the system, and what equipment will be needed.

Environmental engineers may work for private industrial companies, for the

Environmental Protection Agency (EPA), or for engineering consulting firms. Environmental engineers who work for private industrial companies help make sure their companies obey environmental laws. That may mean designing new waste systems or making sure the old ones are operating up to standard. Engineers might, for example, plan a system to move wastewater from the manufacturing process area to a treatment area, and then to a discharge site (a place where the treated wastewater can be pumped out). Engineers might write reports explaining the design. They also might file forms with the government to prove that the company is complying with the laws.

Environmental engineers who work for the EPA might not design the waste treatment systems themselves, but they do have to know how such systems are designed and built. If there is a pollution problem in their area, they need to figure out if a waste control system is causing the problem, and what might have gone wrong.

Environmental engineers working for engineering consulting firms work on many different types of problems.

Exploring

Check your library and bookstore for reading material on engineering and the environment. One journal that may be available in your library is *Chemical & Engineering News,* which regularly features articles on waste management systems. Its Web site address is: http://pubs.acs.org/cen/. Another magazine for environmental engineers is *Pollution Engineering,* which you can also see online at http://www.pollutionengineering.com. There is more information on the subject on Environmental Database, a fun Web site for students at http://www.soton.ac.uk/~engenvir/.

WORDS TO LEARN

Biodegradation: The use of bacteria or other living organisms to decompose contaminants.

CERCLA (Comprehensive Environmental Response, Compensation, and Liability Act): A 1980 law (known as "Superfund") that mandated cleanup of private and government-owned hazardous waste sites.

EPA (U.S. Environmental Protection Agency): The federal agency responsible for overseeing the implementation of environmental laws, including those designed to monitor and control air, water, and soil pollution. State EPAs help carry out these laws.

Hazardous waste: Any discarded substance, usually chemicals, that can cause harm to humans.

National Priorities List: U.S. EPA list of the worst hazardous waste sites in the country needing cleanup.

Remediation: Environmental cleanup.

Septic: Anaerobic (without air) decomposition typically accompanied by an unpleasant odor.

Consulting firms are independent companies that help others comply with environmental laws. They design and build waste control systems for their clients. They also deal with the EPA on behalf of their clients, filling out forms and checking to see what requirements must be met.

Education and Training

You will have to earn a bachelor's degree to work as an environmental engineer. Take as many science and mathematics courses as possible to prepare for college. About 20 colleges offer a bachelor's degree in environmental engineering. Another option is to earn another type of engineering degree such as civil, industrial, or mechanical engineering, with additional courses in environmental engineering.

Earnings

Entry-level salaries for environmental engineers are about $30,000. In water quality management, engineers start at $30,000 to $40,000 for government jobs and $30,000 and up for private jobs. Those in solid waste management earn slightly less than those in hazardous waste management. The U.S. Department of Labor reports that environmental protection specialists in the federal government earned about $58,000 in 1999. The median annual salary of inspectors and compliance officers was $36,820 in 1998.

FOR MORE INFO

American Academy of Environmental Engineers
130 Holiday Court, Suite 100
Annapolis, MD 21401
410-266-3311
http://www.enviro-engrs.org

Junior Engineering Technical Society
1420 King Street
Alexandria, VA 22314
703-548-5387
jets@nae.edu
http://www.jets.org

Student Conservation Association
689 River Road
PO Box 550
Charlestown, NH 03603-0550
603-543-1700
http://www.sca-inc.org

Outlook

Many of the major cleanup efforts of the 1980s were finished by the 1990s, causing the environmental engineering job market to slow down. In the next decade, the water supply and water pollution control specialties will offer the most job opportunities for environmental engineers. Opportunities will be available with all three major employers—the EPA, industry, and consulting firms. The U.S. Department of Labor predicts average growth in employment of inspectors and compliance officials through 2008.

Fish and Game Wardens

Meet Judie Miller, Refuge Ranger

Judie Miller is a refuge ranger and public affairs officer at the Minnesota Valley National Wildlife Refuge in Bloomington, Minnesota. She is responsible for outreach at the refuge, "which means that I need to inform not only the public, but our internal audiences about our mission and what we are doing."

Miller notes that "refuge ranger" is a general title that includes law enforcement workers, environmental educators, public affairs officers and volunteers. "My job also includes handling a number of special events at Minnesota Valley," says Miller. "For example, I coordinate the National Wildlife Refuge Week events at this refuge. I do many other outreach jobs, such as creating and writing newsletters, and press releases, to get word out to people about our refuge."

What Fish and Game Wardens Do

Fish and game wardens are also called *wildlife conservationists, wildlife inspectors, refuge rangers,* and *refuge officers.* They protect wildlife, manage resources, and also perform public information and law enforcement tasks.

The conservation of fish and wildlife is a responsibility that grows more complex each year, especially with growing pollution and environmental changes. To accomplish its mission, the U.S. Fish and Wildlife Service, for example, employs many of the country's best biologists, wildlife managers, engineers, realty specialists, law enforcement agents, and others who work to save endangered and threatened species; conserve migratory birds and inland fisheries; provide expert advice to other federal agencies, industry, and foreign governments; and manage more than 700 offices and field stations. These personnel are working in every state and territory from the Arctic Ocean to the South Pacific, and from the Atlantic to the Caribbean.

Wildlife inspectors and special agents are two jobs that fall in the fish and game warden category of the U.S. Fish and Wildlife Service. Wildlife inspectors monitor the legal trade of federally protected fish and wildlife and intercept illegal imports and exports. At points of entry into the United States, wildlife inspectors examine shipping containers, live animals, wildlife products such as animal skins, and documents. Inspectors, who work closely with special agents, may seize shipments as evidence, conduct investigations, and testify in courts of law.

Special agents of the U.S. Fish and Wildlife Service are trained criminal investigators who enforce federal wildlife laws throughout the country. Special agents conduct investigations, which may include surveillance, undercover work, making arrests, and preparing cases for court. These agents enforce migratory bird regulations and investigate illegal trade in protected wildlife.

Refuge rangers or refuge managers work at the more than 550 national refuges

Exploring

- Visit your local nature centers and park preserves often. Attend any classes or special lectures they offer. There may be opportunities to volunteer to help clean up sites, plant trees, or maintain pathways and trails.
- Get to know your local wildlife. What kind of insects, birds, fish, and other animals live in your area?
- Here are some reading suggestions:
And Then There Was One: The Mysteries of Extinction by Margery Facklam (Little Brown & Co., 1993).
The National Wildlife Federation's Wildlife Watcher's Handbook: A Guide to Observing Animals in the Wild by Joe La Tourrette (Owlet, 1997).
The Wildlife Detectives: How Forensic Scientists Fight Crimes Against Nature by Donna M. Jackson, Wendy Shattil, and Robert Rozinski (Houghton Miflin Co., 2000).

across the country, protecting and conserving migratory and native species of birds, mammals, fish, endangered species, and other wildlife. Many of these refuges also offer outdoor recreational opportunities and educational programs.

Education and Training

Courses in biology and other sciences, geography, mathematics, social studies, and physical education will help you prepare for this career.

To become a fish and game warden you must have a bachelor's degree or three years of work experience. Higher positions require at least one year of graduate studies and some professional positions, such as biologist or manager, require master's or doctoral degrees.

GOVERNMENTS STEP IN TO CURB EXTINCTION

For centuries, wildlife has suffered because of the actions of human beings. Bows, rifles, and shotguns made it easier for people to kill game. ("Game" is any fish, birds, or mammals that are hunted nongame.) Some species of animals have been commercially for food, sport, or both.) Some species of animals have been hunted to extinction. Forests have been cleared, swamps drained, and rivers dammed to clear the way for agriculture and industry. These activities have harmed or destroyed large areas of plant and wildlife habitat.

Beginning in the late 19th century, there was growing concern for vanishing wildlife. The governments of the United States and other nations started conservation programs and passed laws to protect wildlife and set aside national parks and other reserves.

The main agency assigned to the conservation of animals and their habitats in this country is the U.S. Fish and Wildlife Service, created in 1856. It is responsible for the scientific development of commercial fisheries and the conservation of fish and wildlife.

On-the-job training is given for most positions. Special agents receive 18 weeks of formal training in criminal investigation and wildlife law enforcement techniques at the Federal Law Enforcement Training Center in Glynco, Georgia.

Earnings

In the wide variety of positions available at the U.S. Fish and Wildlife Service, salaries range from $18,000 up to $91,000 for more advanced positions. Law enforcement positions, especially special agents, receive higher salaries because their jobs are more dangerous.

Outlook

The largest number of jobs in the field are with the U.S. Fish and Wildlife Service and other agencies of the Department of the Interior, such as the National Park Service. State agencies, such as Departments of Natural Resources or Departments of Parks and Recreation, also have positions in this area.

> **FOR MORE INFO**
>
> *You can learn more about fish and game wardens and related employment opportunities through the following organizations:*
>
> **U.S. Fish and Wildlife Service**
> Department of the Interior
> 1849 C Street, NW
> Washington, DC 20240
> 703-358-2120
> http://www.fws.gov
>
> **U.S. National Park Service**
> Department of the Interior
> 1849 C Street, NW
> Washington, DC 20240
> 202-208-6843
> http://www.nps.gov

Employment growth in this field depends on politics and government. Some administrations spend more on wildlife concerns, while others make cutbacks in this area.

RELATED JOBS

Biologists
Ecologists
Naturalists
Park Rangers
Range Managers

Foresters

A Better Way to Plant

Foresters and woodland owners often renew harvested forest areas by planting seeds or seedlings of particular kinds of trees. These seedlings are usually grown in large nurseries and transplanted when they are hardy and old enough to survive.

When companies first began replanting harvested forests, all of the planting was done by hand. Since the 1940s, however, the replanting has been done increasingly by a tree-planting machine. As the planting machine is pulled behind a tractor, a plow-like blade cuts open a furrow in the ground. A forestry worker places the seedlings in the ground by hand. Wheels on the planting machine close the furrow around the seedling. Machine planting allows a crew to plant thousands of seedlings in one day.

What Foresters Do

Foresters protect and manage forests. They map the locations of resources, such as timber, game shelter, food, snow, and water. Foresters also identify areas that need treatment, which may include planting trees, controlling diseases or insects, scattering seeds, or pruning trees. Foresters lay out logging roads or roads to lakes and campgrounds. Some foresters make the plans for building campgrounds and shelters, supervise crews, and inspect the work after it is done.

Foresters select and mark trees to be cut. They are in charge of the lookouts, patrols, and pilots who watch for fires. They also lead crews that fight fires. Some foresters supervise campgrounds, find lost hikers, and rescue climbers and skiers.

Foresters must record the work done in the forest on maps and in reports. Sometimes they use computers and data processing equipment. They also use aer-

A forester inspects the progress at a logging site.

ial photography. Some foresters work in the laboratories and factories of wood-related industries, such as sawmills, pulp and paper mills, wood preserving plants, and furniture factories. Others do research in laboratories, greenhouses, and forests.

Foresters may specialize. For example, *silviculturists* specialize in the establishment and reproduction of forests. They regulate forest makeup, and manage forest growth and development. *Forest engineers* design and construct roads, bridges, dams, and buildings in forest areas. These construction projects help the movement of logs and pulpwood out of the forest. *Forest ecologists* conduct research to determine how forests are affected by changes in environmental conditions, such as light, soil, climate, altitude, and animals.

EXPLORING

• Visit local forest preserves often. Most preserves offer education programs and workshops. Some may have volunteer programs.

• In some parts of the country, local chapters of the Society of American Foresters invite prospective forestry students to some of their meetings and field trips. (See For More Info.)

Education and Training

A professional forester must graduate from a four-year school of forestry with a bachelor's degree. Some foresters have master's degrees. Most schools of forestry are part of state universities. In forestry school, you learn how to tend and reproduce forests. In addition, you study forest economics and the harvesting and marketing of forest crops. You work in the forest as a part of your university training.

Earnings

According to the U.S. Department of Labor, conservation scientists and foresters earned about $42,700 in 1998. Salaries ranged from less than $26,300 to more than $75,300.

In 1999, most bachelor's degree graduates entering federal government jobs as foresters, range managers, or soil conservationists earned from $20,600 to $25,500, depending on college records. Those with master's degrees earned $25,500 to $31,200 to start and those with doctorates started at $37,700. In 1999, foresters working for the federal government earned

FOREST FACTS

- It has been estimated that Americans come in contact with more than 10,000 items each day that have come from forests.
- Most forest fires are now detected by aircraft or closed-circuit television, rather than the traditional lookout towers.
- The largest forest area in the United States is the Central Hardwood Forest, which stretches across eastern North America and encompasses part or all of 28 U.S. states and two Canadian provinces.
- Most hardwoods are deciduous, which means they lose their leaves each fall. Most softwoods are evergreens, which mean they lose only some of their needles each year and remain green year-round.
- Older, slower-growing trees and trees that have been damaged by fire or drought are most vulnerable to attack by disease and insects.

average salaries of about $51,000.

Outlook

More than half of the foresters working in the United States are employed by government agencies, such as the Forest Service, the Bureau of Land Management, or the National Park Service, as well as state and local agencies. Many foresters also work in private industry.

Job opportunities in forestry are expected to increase about as fast as the average through 2008. Budget cuts in federal programs have limited hiring. Also, federal land management agencies, such as the Forest Service, are giving less attention to timber programs and are focusing more on wildlife, recreation, and sustaining ecosystems.

There have also been cutbacks in timber harvesting on public lands, most of which are located in the Northwest and California, also affecting job growth for private industry foresters. Opportunities will be better for foresters on privately owned land in the Southeast. Landowners and industries, such as paper companies, sawmills, and pulp wood mills will continue to need foresters.

For More Info

American Forests
PO Box 2000
Washington, DC 20013
202-955-4500
http://www.amfor.org

Society of American Foresters
5400 Grosvenor Lane
Bethesda, MD 20814
301-897-8720
http://www.safnet.org

USDA Forest Service
2nd Floor, Central Wing
PO Box 96090
Washington, DC 20090-6090
202-205-8333
http://www.fs.fed.us

Canadian Forestry Association
185 Somerset Street West, Suite 203
Ottawa, ON K2P OJ2 Canada
613-232-1815

Geologists

Rock-Collecting Tips

Many people collect rocks as a hobby. Some gather them for color, such as agate with its bands of many hues. Others collect specimens for odd or beautiful shapes. Some look for imprints of fossils. Some gather historic rocks, such as stones from battlefields or Indian mounds.

For people who want to do their own collecting, every part of the country offers specimens. Mountains, seashores, river banks, woods, and lava plains are especially abundant in varied rocks. Many people simply pick up rocks on the surface of the ground. Others carry rock hammers, picks, nippers, and Geiger counters. Hobbyists can buy rocks from specialty stores or scientific supply houses.

What Geologists Do

Geologists study the earth—how it was formed, what it is made of, and how it is slowly changing. They take rock samples. Generally, geologists spend three to six months of the year making maps of certain areas and drilling deep holes in the earth to obtain these rock samples. They study the rock samples in their laboratories under controlled temperatures and pressures. Finally, they organize the information they have gathered and write reports. These reports may be used to locate groundwater, oil, minerals, and other natural resources.

Many geologists specialize in a particular study of the earth. For example, those who study the oceans are called *marine geologists.* Those who try to locate natural gas and oil deposits are called *petroleum geologists. Paleontologists* study the earth's rock formations to determine the age of the earth.

Chipping through layers of rock, geologists study the structure and types of rocks found in an area.

Geologists' work can be physically demanding. They travel often and spend a lot of time in remote and rugged areas. In addition, they spend long hours in the laboratory and preparing reports.

Most geologists work in private businesses. More than half of them work for oil and gas companies in the field of exploration. The federal government hires geologists to work in the Department of the Interior (the U.S. Geological Survey, the Bureau of Mines, or the Bureau of Reclamation) and in the Departments of Defense, Agriculture, and Commerce. Geologists also work for state agencies, research organizations, universities, and museums.

EXPLORING

- Amateur geological groups and local museums may have geology clubs you can join.
- Here are some reading suggestions:
Geology Crafts for Kids: 50 Nifty Projects to Explore the Marvels of Planet Earth by Alan Anderson (Lark Books, 1996).
Rocks and Minerals by Gracy Staedter (Reader's Digest Children's Publishing, 1999).
Geology: The Active Earth by Sandra Stotsky (The McGraw Hill Companies, 1996).

What Do Geological Technicians Do?

Geological technicians help geologists study the earth's physical makeup and history. This includes the exploration of mountain uplifting, rock formations, mineral deposits, earthquakes, and volcanoes.

Petroleum technicians measure and record the conditions of oil and gas wells. They use instruments lowered into the wells, and evaluate mud from the wells. They examine data to determine petroleum and mineral content.

Geological technicians most often work as part of a research team. The most common employment for geological technicians is with petroleum geologists. These scientists determine where deposits of oil and natural gas may be buried beneath the earth's surface. Geological technicians draw maps to show where drilling operations are taking place. They write reports that geologists use to determine where an oil deposit might be located.

Geological technicians also draw maps that show exactly where a drilling crew has dug a well. The map tells whether or not oil was found and specifies the depth of the well.

Some geological technicians work in the field of environmental engineering. They help geologists study how structures, such as roads, landfills, and buildings affect the environment.

Education and Training

To be a geologist, you need to earn a bachelor's degree, usually in the physical and earth sciences. Positions in research, teaching, or exploration require a master's degree. Geologists who want to teach in a college or university or head a department in a commercial business must earn a doctorate.

Many colleges, universities, and technical institutes offer programs in geology. Besides courses in geology, students study physics, chemistry, mathematics, English composition, economics, and foreign languages. Students who go on to graduate school will take advanced courses in geology and in the specialization of their choice.

FOR MORE INFO

American Geological Institute
4220 King Street
Alexandria, VA 22302
703-379-2480
http://www.agiweb.org

Geological Society of America
300 Penrose Place
Boulder, CO 80301-9140
303-447-2020
http://www.geosociety.org

Earnings

Beginning geologists earn about $34,900 a year, on the average. Those with master's degrees earn $44,700. More experienced geologists can earn as much as $60,000 to $90,000 a year. Geologists who work for the federal government generally earn less.

Outlook

The U.S. Department of Labor predicts that employment of geologists will have average growth through 2008.

Geologists will find jobs in the petroleum industry, but competition for those jobs will be strong. Many of these positions may be in foreign countries. Geologists may also find jobs in environmental protection and reclamation (cleanup).

RELATED JOBS

Ecologists
Environmental Engineers
Geological Technicians
Geophysicists
Groundwater Professionals
Oceanographers
Petroleum Engineers
Petrologists

Hazardous Waste Management Technicians

Hazards of Household Waste

Americans produce 1.6 million tons of household hazardous waste per year, according to the U.S. EPA. The average home stores as much as 100 pounds of household hazardous waste in its basement, garage, and closets. Products containing hazardous ingredients may include paints, cleaners, stains and varnishes, car batteries, motor oil, and pesticides. The used or leftover portions of these products is known as household hazardous waste. Sometimes people dispose of this waste improperly. They may pour it down the drain, on the ground, into storm sewers, or throw it in the trash. All of these practices can be dangerous. Instead, follow instructions on the label for proper disposal or take household hazardous waste to a proper collection facility.

What Hazardous Waste Management Technicians Do

It takes many different professionals to clean up hazardous waste sites—scientists, engineers, specialists, technicians, and others. *Hazardous waste management technicians* are part of this team that identifies waste sites and remediates, or cleans up, waste. Hazardous materials are defined by the Environmental Protection Agency (EPA) as those harmful to the environment or health. Technicians take water or soil samples to test for the presence of hazardous materials that have leaked, spilled, or been dumped into the environment.

Some hazardous waste technicians may be specially trained in emergency response procedures. Hazardous waste emergencies may occur when a chemical plant has a leak or an explosion or when

A hazardous waste management technician tests water and soil samples for evidence of pollution.

a semi-trailer or train carrying a hazardous substance is involved in an accident. Hazardous waste technicians are among the first people sent to sites that pose immediate health risks to the general public.

More often, hazardous waste management technicians help identify and clean up sites that have already been contaminated and don't pose an immediate danger. One of the first duties of a technician on a site is to observe the environment. Can the effects of the hazardous material be seen? What type of material is it? The technicians perform an exact analysis of

EXPLORING

Here are some resources to help you learn more about hazardous waste management:

The Encyclopedia of the Environment by Stephen Keller and Matthew Black, eds. (Franklin Watts, 1999).

Environmental Database
http://www.soton.ac.uk/~engenvir

Hazardous Waste Clean-Up Information
http://clu-in.com

the soil or groundwater that might be contaminated. They take samples in the field and perform laboratory tests. They may have to take samples many times. Technicians give their data to specialists in hazardous waste management who plan how to clean up the site.

Education and Training

Students interested in a career in hazardous waste management should concentrate on science courses, especially chemistry, biology, and geology. Computers, mathematics, speech, and communications will also be helpful.

You need at least a high school diploma to become a hazardous waste management technician. For most hazardous waste jobs, postsecondary training is required because of new safety considerations and new treatment technologies. Two-year associate's degrees in hazardous waste management or environmental resource management are available from many

WASTE TREATMENT TECHNOLOGIES

Biological treatment, or **bioremediation,** uses bacteria, fungi, or algae to remove and break down the hazardous substances.

Chemical reduction uses strong reducing agents, such as sulfur dioxide, alkali salts, sulfides, and iron salts, to break down hazardous substances and make them less toxic.

Incineration is the high-temperature burning of a waste, usually at 1,600 to 2,500 degrees F.

Microencapsulation is a process that coats the surface of the waste material with a thin layer of plastic or resin to prevent the material from leaching waste substances.

Stabilization reduces the mobility of hazardous substances in a waste and makes the waste easier to handle. Common stabilization agents are Portland cement, lime, fly ash, and cement kiln dust.

technical institutes and community colleges. These schools and some organizations offer workshops to keep employees up to date on current technological and legal aspects of the career.

Earnings

Salaries for hazardous waste management technicians, or science technicians, as they are classified by the government, earned about $31,000 a year in 1998. Salaries ranged from $19,000 to $50,000 a year. Science technicians who worked for the federal government earned between $16,400 and $20,600 to start.

Outlook

There is no shortage of contaminated sites for hazardous waste technicians to work on. Technician jobs are fairly secure, but the hazardous waste management industry continues to change. The cleanup of sites is usually very costly and depends on funding by the government. Public pressure to clean up sites has kept environmental funding steady over the years, though. The U.S. Department of Labor predicts that the demand will continue for technicians to help regulate waste products; collect air, water, and soil samples for measuring pollution levels; monitor compliance with regulations; and clean up contaminated sites.

FOR MORE INFO

The Institute of Hazardous Materials Management
11900 Parklawn Drive, Suite 450
Rockville, MD 20852
301-984-8969
http://www.ihmm.org

National Partnership for Environmental Technology in Education
6601 Owens Drive, Suite 235
Pleasanton, CA 94588
510-225-0668

U.S. Army Corps of Engineers
20 Massachusetts Avenue, NW
Washington, DC 20314-1000
202-761-0660
http://www.usace.army.mil/

Land Trust or Preserve Managers

What Land Trust or Preserve Managers Do

Land trusts, owned by private organizations, and preserves, government-owned lands, are protected from being developed, polluted, mined, too heavily farmed, or otherwise damaged. Hundreds of millions of acres of land and water are protected in land trusts or preserves.

Preserve managers work for the federal government, which owns more than 700 million acres, about one-third of the United States, including forests, wilderness areas, wildlife refuges, scenic rivers, and other sites. Most of this land is managed by agencies, such as the National Park Service, U.S. Fish and Wildlife Service, and Forest Service. State and local governments also may own and manage preserve lands. The federal government employs about 75 percent of all people working in land and water conservation.

The Unlucky 13

In March 2001, the Nature Conservancy announced the creation of Prairie Wings, a program to protect, manage, and restore the grassland bird habitat of the central United States, south-central Canada, and north-central Mexico. Grassland bird populations have declined more steeply and consistently over a wider area than any other group of vertebrate animals in North America. The Conservancy named 13 species, called the "Unlucky 13," that are especially in danger:

Greater prairie chicken
Lesser prairie chicken
Long-billed curlew
Ferruginous hawk
Lark bunting
Chestnut-collared longspur
McCown's longspur
Burrowing owl
Sprague's pipit
Mountain plover
Baird's sparrow
Cassin's sparrow
Scaled quail

A preserve manager teaches a group about the preserve's conservation work.

Land trust managers work for private, nonprofit land trusts. Land trusts have become an important way for citizens concerned about the environment to take action. For example, in the 1970s, a land trust saved miles of San Francisco coastline from development. Land trusts get land by buying it, accepting it as a donation, or purchasing the development rights to it. There are about 1,100 land trusts in the United States today. Land trusts can be small; one person might do everything. A few land trusts have a large, paid staff of 30 or more.

Land trust and preserve managers plan for recreational use of land and water.

Exploring

• Ask your librarian to help you find books on prairie, wetland, riparian (river bank), and wildlife conservation.

• Contact nonprofit land trusts or federal agencies for information about current projects in your area.

TEDDY AND THE ENVIRONMENT

One of the most important people in early conservation efforts was the 26th president of the United States, Theodore Roosevelt. He fell in love with the West as a young man, when illness led him there to seek better air. He owned a ranch in the Dakota Territory and wrote many books about his experiences in the West.

When he became president in 1901, Roosevelt used his influence to help preserve his beloved West. He pushed conservation as part of an overall strategy for the responsible use of natural resources, including forests, pastures, fish, game, soil, and minerals. This increased public awareness of and support for conservation and led to important early conservation legislation. Roosevelt's administration especially emphasized the preservation of forests, wildlife, park lands, wilderness areas, and watershed areas and carried out such work as the first inventory of natural resources in this country.

They take inventory of plant and animal species and protect wildlife habitats. They clean up pollution and restore damaged ecosystems. They manage forests, prairies, rangelands, and wetlands using techniques such as controlled burnings and grazing by bison or cattle.

Education and Training

A background in biology, chemistry, and physics is important for land trust or preserve managers. A bachelor's degree in a natural science, such as zoology, biology, or botany, is recommended. A master's or a doctorate in a specialty also is a good idea, especially for government positions.

Land trusts need people who are good in business to run the trusts, raise funds, negotiate deals, and handle tax matters. The large land trust organizations also need lawyers, public relations specialists, and others.

Earnings

The National Association of Colleges and Employers reports that graduates with a bachelor's degree in natural resources received average starting salary offers of $26,100.

The salary range for conservation professionals is about $20,600 to $25,500 for entry-level jobs. Average salaries are about $42,750. Conservation professionals with master's degrees and experience earn from $50,000 to $75,300 a year.

Outlook

Right now, the best opportunities are with private land trusts and national land trust organizations, rather than federal agencies. None of the federal agencies is expected to see big growth over the next few years. Private land trusts, however, are growing.

Land trusts are the fastest growing area of the conservation movement today. According to the Land Trust Alliance, there were approximately 1,213 land trusts in 1998. LTA's 1998 National Land Trust Census reports that local and regional land trusts protected 4.7 million acres, 135 percent more than just a decade earlier.

FOR MORE INFO

Land Trust Alliance
1331 H Street, NW, Suite 400
Washington, DC 20005
202-638-4725
http://www.lta.org

The following organization specializes in land trusts and land trust management for areas with rare or endangered species.
The Nature Conservancy
4245 North Fairfax Drive, Suite 100
Arlington VA 22203-1606
800-628-6860
http://www.nature.org

SCA's monthly publication, Earth Work, *includes job listings.*
Student Conservation Association
PO Box 550
Charlestown, NH 03603
ask-us@sca-inc.org
603-543-1828
http://www.sca-inc.org

Naturalists

The Beginnings of Conservation

During the 19th century in the United States, many great forests were cut down and huge areas of land were leveled for open-pit mining and quarrying. More disease occurred with the increase of air pollution from the smokestacks of factories, home chimneys, and engine exhaust. At the same time there was a dramatic decrease in populations of elk, antelope, deer, bison, and other animals of the Great Plains. Some types of bear, cougar, and wolf became extinct, as well as several kinds of birds, such as the passenger pigeon. In the latter half of the 19th century, the government set up a commission to develop scientific management of fisheries. It established the first national park (Yellowstone National Park in Wyoming), and set aside the first forest reserves. These early steps led to the modern conservation movement.

What Naturalists Do

Naturalists study the natural world in order to learn the best way to preserve the earth and its living creatures—humans, animals, and plants. They teach the public about the environment and show people what they can do about such hazards as pollution.

Naturalists may work in wildlife museums, private nature centers, or large zoos. Some naturalists work for parks, most of which are operated by state or federal governments. Naturalists also can work as *nature resource managers, wildlife conservationists, ecologists,* and *environmental educators* for many different employers.

Depending on where they work, naturalists may protect and conserve wildlife or particular kinds of land, such as prairie or wetlands. Other naturalists research and carry out plans to restore lands that have been damaged by erosion, fire, or devel-

In the Everglades, this naturalist uses binoculars to view the many species of birds to be identified for a wetland report.

opment. Some naturalists re-create wildlife habitats and nature trails. They plant trees, for example, or label existing plants. *Fish and wildlife wardens* help regulate populations of fish, hunted animals, and protected animals. They control hunting and fishing and make sure species are thriving but not overpopulating their territories. *Wildlife managers, range managers,* and *conservationists* also maintain the plant and animal life in a certain area. They work in parks or on ranges that have both domestic livestock and wild animals. They test soil and water for nutrients and pollution. They count plant and animal populations each season.

Naturalists do some indoor work. They raise funds for projects, write reports,

EXPLORING

- Visit your local nature centers and park preserves often. Attend any classes or special lectures they offer. There may be opportunities to volunteer to help clean up sites, plant trees, or maintain pathways and trails.
- Hiking, birdwatching, and photography are good hobbies for future naturalists.
- Get to know your local wildlife. What kind of insects, birds, fish, and other animals live in your area? Your librarian will be able to help you find books that identify local flora and fauna.

keep detailed records, and write articles, brochures, and newsletters to educate the public about their work. They might campaign for support for protection of an endangered species by holding meetings and hearings. Other public education activities include giving tours and nature walks and holding demonstrations, exhibits, and classes.

Education and Training

Naturalists must have at least a bachelor's degree in biology, zoology, chemistry, botany, natural history, or environmental science. A master's degree is not a requirement, but is useful, and many naturalists have a master's degree in education. Experience gained through summer jobs and volunteer work can be just as important as educational requirements. Experience working with the public is also helpful.

Earnings

Starting salaries for full-time naturalists range from about

SOME PIONEER NATURALISTS

Ralph Waldo Emerson (1803-1882) was an American philosopher and author. He helped form and promote the philosophy known as Transcendentalism, which emphasizes the spiritual dimension in nature and in all persons.

Henry David Thoreau (1817-1862) was an American author. His *Walden* (1854) is a classic of American literature. It tells about the two years he lived in a small cabin on the shore of Walden Pond near Concord, Massachusetts. In *Walden*, he described the changing seasons and other natural events and scenes that he observed.

Gilbert White (1720-1793) was an English minister. While living and working in his native village of Selborne (southwest of London), White became a careful observer of its natural setting. He corresponded with important British naturalists and eventually published *The Natural History and Antiquities of Selborne*.

$15,000 to $22,000 per year. Some part-time workers, however, make as little as minimum wage ($5.15 per hour). For some positions, housing and vehicles may be provided. Earnings vary for those with added responsibilities or advanced degrees. Field officers and supervisors make between $25,000 and $45,000 a year, and upper management employees can earn between $30,000 and $70,000.

Outlook

In the next decade, the job outlook for naturalists is expected to be only fair, despite the public's increasing environmental awareness. Private nature centers and preserves—where forests, wetlands, and prairies are restored—are continuing to open in the United States, but possible government cutbacks in nature programs may limit their growth. Competition will be quite strong, since there are many qualified people entering this field.

FOR MORE INFO

Contact the following organizations for more information on a career as a naturalist:

Bureau of Land Management
U.S. Department of the Interior
1849 C Street, Room 406-LS
Washington, DC 20240
http://www.blm.gov

Environmental Careers Organization
179 South Street
Boston, MA 02111
http://www.eco.org

This group has an international computer network called EcoNet that features electronic bulletin boards on environmental issues, services, events, news, and job listings.

Institute for Global Communication
18 DeBoom Street
San Francisco, CA 94107
415-442-0220
http://www.econet.org

National Wildlife Federation
8925 Leesburg Pike
Vienna, VA 22184
718-790-4000
http://www.nwf.org

North American Association for Environmental Education
410 Tarvin Road
Rock Spring, GA 30739
706-764-2926
http://naaee.org/

Oceanographers

What Oceanographers Do

Oceanographers study the oceans. They perform experiments and gather information about the water, plant and animal life, and the ocean floor. They study the motion of waves, currents, and tides. They also look at water temperature, chemical makeup of the ocean water, oil deposits on the ocean floor, and pollution levels at different depths of the oceans.

Oceanographers use several inventions specially designed for long- and short-term underwater observation. They use deep-sea equipment, such as submarines and observation tanks. Underwater devices called *bathyspheres* allow an oceanographer to stay underwater for several hours or even days. For short observations or to explore areas such as underwater caves, scientists use deep-sea and scuba diving

Oceans of the World

Name	Square Miles	Greatest Depth
Pacific	64,186,300	35,810
Atlantic	33,420,000	28,232
Indian	28,350,500	25,344
Arctic	5,105,700	18,399

The area figures for the oceans include all adjoining seas, so that all the continuous saltwater (the world ocean) is included. For example, the Mediterranean and Black seas are included in the Atlantic Ocean. The Bering and China seas are included in the Pacific Ocean. The Arabian Sea is included in the Indian Ocean.

The Floating Instrument Platform, FLIP, is a 395-foot-long nonpropelled research platform used to support a variety of oceanographic research projects.

gear that straps onto the body to supply them with oxygen.

Oceanographers do most of their work out on the water. While at sea, they gather the scientific information that they need. Then they spend months or years in offices, laboratories, or libraries examining the data. Oceanographers use information such as water temperature changes between the surface and the lower depths to predict droughts and monsoon rains.

Most oceanographers specialize in one of four areas. Those who study ocean

EXPLORING

If you live near coastal regions, it will be easier to become familiar with oceans and ocean life. Read all you can about rocks, minerals, or aquatic life. If you live or travel near an oceanography research center, such as Woods Hole Oceanographic Institution on Cape Cod in Massachusetts, spend some time studying their exhibits.

If you do not live near water, try to find summer camps or programs that make trips to coastal areas. Learn all you can about the geology, atmosphere, and plant and animal life of the area where you live, regardless of whether water is present.

NATURE 51

DID YOU KNOW?

- Oceans cover nearly three-quarters of the planet's surface—336 million cubic miles.
- Ocean depth averages 2.3 miles. The greatest known depth of any ocean is in the Challenger Deep of the Mariana Trench in the Pacific Ocean, about 250 miles southwest of Guam. Recorded echo soundings show a maximum depth of about 36,000 feet.
- The ocean's intricate food webs support more life by weight and a greater diversity of animals than any other ecosystem.
- The oceans have vast stores of valuable minerals, including nickel, iron, manganese, copper, and cobalt.
- The surface temperature of oceans ranges from about 86 degrees F at the equator to about 29 degrees F near the poles. The world's warmest water is in the Persian Gulf, where surface temperatures of 96 degrees F have been recorded.

Physical oceanographers study ocean temperature and the atmosphere above the water. They study the greenhouse effect, or the warming of the planet's surface. They calculate the movement of the warm water through the oceans to help meteorologists predict weather patterns.

Geological oceanographers study the ocean floor. They use instruments that monitor the ocean floor and the minerals found there from a far distance. In areas where the ocean is too deep for any manmade equipment to go, they use remote sensors.

Geochemical oceanographers study the chemical makeup of ocean water and the ocean floor. They detect oil well sites. They study pollution problems and possible chemical causes for plant and animal diseases in a particular region of the water. Geochemical oceanographers

plants and animals are called *biological oceanographers* or *marine biologists.* They collect information on the behavior and activities of the wildlife in a specific area of the ocean water.

are called in after oil spills to check the level of damage to the water.

Education and Training

To become an oceanographer, you will need at least a bachelor's degree in chemistry, biology, geology, or physics. For most research or teaching positions, you will need a master's degree or doctoral degree in oceanography.

Earnings

Entry-level salaries in oceanography for those with bachelor's degrees average about $34,900 a year. An average annual salary for experienced oceanographers is around $66,000, with the highest paid making up to $100,000 a year.

Outlook

Jobs for oceanographers can change according to the world market situation. The state of the offshore oil market, for instance, can affect the demand for geophysical oceanographers. The growing interest in understanding and protecting the environment will help to create new jobs. There will be more opportunities in global climate change, environmental research, fisheries science, and biomedical and pharmaceutical research.

FOR MORE INFO

For a booklet on marine-related careers, send a check or money order for $6 to:
Marine Technology Society
1828 L Street, NW, Suite 906
Washington, DC 20036
202-775-5966

For a 24-page color brochure entitled "Careers in Oceanography and Marine-Related Fields," contact:
The Oceanography Society
5912 LeMay Road
Rockville, MD 20851-2326
301-881-1101
http://www.tos.org

Scripps Institute of Oceanography
0-233 University of California, San Diego
9500 Gilman Drive
La Jolla, CA 92093-0233
http://www.sio.ucsd.edu

Park Rangers

Our National Parks

The National Park System in the United States was begun by Congress in 1872 when Yellowstone National Park was created. The National Park Service, a bureau of the U.S. Department of the Interior, was created in 1916 to preserve, protect, and manage the national, cultural, historical, and recreational areas of the National Park System. At that time, the entire park system was less than 1 million acres. Today, the country's national parks cover more than 80 million acres of mountains, plains, deserts, swamps, historic sites, lakeshores, forests, rivers, battlefields, memorials, archaeological properties, and recreation areas.

What Park Rangers Do

Park rangers protect animals and preserve forests, ponds, and other natural resources in state and national parks. They teach visitors about the park by giving lectures and tours. They also enforce rules and regulations to maintain a safe environment for visitors and wildlife.

One of the most important responsibilities park rangers have is safety. Rangers often require visitors to register at park offices so they will know when the visitors are expected to return from a hike or other activity. Rangers are trained in first aid and, if there is an accident, they may have to help visitors who have been injured. Rangers carefully mark hiking trails and other areas to lessen the risk of injuries for visitors and to protect plants and animals.

Rangers help visitors enjoy and learn about parks. They give lectures and provide guided tours of the park, explaining

Many accidents occur in national parks. For that reason, rangers must be trained in first aid and emergency care.

why certain plants and animals live there. They explain about the rocks and soil in the area and point out important historical sites.

Research and conservation efforts are also a big part of a park ranger's responsibilities. They study wildlife behavior by tagging and following certain animals. They may investigate sources of pollution that come from outside the park. Then they develop plans to help reduce pollution to make the park a better place for plants, animals, and visitors.

Rangers also do bookkeeping and other paperwork. They issue permits to visitors and keep track of how many people use the park. They also plan recreational activities and decide how to spend the money budgeted to the park.

EXPLORING

• You may be able to volunteer at national, state, or county parks. Universities and conservation organizations often have volunteer groups that work on research activities, studies, and rehabilitation efforts.

• Get to know your local wildlife. What kind of insects, birds, fish, and other animals live in your area? Your librarian will be able to help you find books that identify local flora and fauna.

NATURE 55

PARKS IN DANGER

The National Parks Conservation Association listed the 10 most endangered national parks in 2000. The names of the parks are followed by their major threats.

Yellowstone National Park: Snowmobiles, which cause noise, ground, and air pollution.

Denali National Park: Proposal to open access by snowmobiles. Road and resort development.

Joshua Tree National Park: Proposed landfill site 1.5 miles outside the park.

Haleakala National Park: Introduction of non-native organisms that threaten rare plants and animals.

Everglades and Biscayne National Parks, and Big Cypress National Preserve: Damage from water management. Off-road vehicle use. Proposed airport development.

Petrified Forest National Park: Visitors taking an estimated 12 tons of fossilized wood annually.

Stones River National Battlefield: Proposed highway and commercial development.

National Underground Railroad Network to Freedom: Lack of funding for buying private property needed for the preservation of this network of sites.

Great Smoky Mountains National Park: Air pollution from regional power-generating plants and motor vehicles.

Ozarks Scenic Riverways National Park: Mining in the surrounding Mark Twain National Forest.

Education and Training

Park rangers usually have bachelor's degrees in natural resource or recreational resource management. A degree in many other fields is also acceptable, such as biology or ecology. Classes in forestry, geology, outdoor management, history, geography, behavioral sciences, and botany are helpful.

Without a degree, you need at least three years of experience working in parks or conservation. You must know about protecting plants and animals and enjoy working outdoors. You also need a pleasant personality and the ability to work with many different kinds of people. You should be good at explaining the natural environment and be able to enforce park rules and regulations. Rangers also receive on-the-job training.

Earnings

Rangers in the National Park Service usually earn starting salaries of around $22,000 a year. More experienced or educated rangers earn approximately $33,000 a year. The government may provide housing to park rangers who work in remote areas.

Outlook

The number of people who want to become park rangers has always been far greater than the number of positions available. The National Park Service has reported that as many as 100 people apply for each job opening. This trend should continue into the future, and because of this stiff competition for positions, the job outlook is expected to change little. Besides the National Park Service, there are some job opportunities in other federal land and resource management agencies and similar state and local agencies.

FOR MORE INFO

National Parks Conservation Association
1300 19th Street, NW, Suite 300
Washington, DC 20036
202-223-6722
http://www.npca.org

National Recreation and Park Association
22377 Belmont Ridge Road
Ashburn, VA 20148-4510
703-858-0784
http://www.nrpa.org

Student Conservation Association
PO Box 550
Charlestown, NH 03603-0550
Tel: 603-543-1700
http://www.sca-inc.org

Pollution Control Technicians

Pollution Solution

One creative solution to control pollution is phytoremediation. Phytoremediation is the use of plants and trees to clean up contaminated soil and water. Plants can break down organic pollutants or stabilize metal contaminants by acting as filters or traps. Over time, plants soak up contaminants from the soil or water into their root systems.

Phytoremediation is being used in Chernobyl, Ukraine, the site of a 1986 nuclear accident. Sunflowers floating on rafts with their roots dangling in water are removing cesium 137 and strontium 90 from a pond. In the eastern United States, where acid mine drainage is a problem, the Bureau of Mines encourages the planting of wetlands using the common cattail to soak up mining contaminants from streams.

What Pollution Control Technicians Do

Pollution control technicians are sometimes called *environmental technicians.* They test water, air, or soil for contamination by pollutants. They work in laboratories and outdoors to find and control air, soil, water, and noise pollution. Most pollution control technicians specialize in one type of pollution.

Water pollution control technicians collect samples of water from rivers, lakes, and other bodies of water or from wastewater. They perform chemical tests that show if it is contaminated, or polluted. In addition to testing the water, technicians may set up equipment to monitor water over a period of time to see if it is becoming polluted. Some technicians test water temperature, pressure, flow, and other characteristics.

Air pollution control technicians collect and analyze samples of gas emissions (smoke) and the atmosphere. They try to find out how badly exhaust fumes from

A pollution control technician checks equipment that monitors pollution emissions from a factory.

automobiles are polluting the air, or whether the smoke from industrial plants contains hazardous pollution. They often set up monitoring equipment outdoors to take air samples or they may try to create the same conditions in a laboratory.

Soil or land pollution control technicians collect soil, silt, or mud samples so they can be checked for contamination. Soil can be contaminated when polluted water or waste seeps into the earth.

Noise pollution control technicians use rooftop devices and mobile units to check

EXPLORING

• Read technical and general-interest publications in environmental science.
• Visit a municipal health department or pollution control agency in your community.
• Tour a local manufacturing plant that uses air- or water-pollution abatement systems.

> # EPA LAWS
>
> As late as the 1950s, there were few pollution control technicians. Environmental laws passed in the 1960s and later created the need for professionals to monitor and regulate pollution of soil, water, and air.
>
> **The Clean Air Act** (1970) regulates air emissions from factories and other sources. The act sets maximum pollutant standards, mainly for industry. For example, if smokestacks at a factory are found to emit pollutants beyond the maximum allowed, the government fines the factory and requires it to reduce emissions by installing scrubbers, changing their processes, or using other solutions.
>
> **The Pollution Prevention Act** (1990) encourages industry, government, and the public to reduce the amount of pollution by making better use of raw materials. The focus is on reducing the amount of waste or pollution produced in the first place, rather than trying to clean it up later. Practices encouraged include recycling, source reduction, and sustainable agriculture. For more information on anti-pollution laws, visit the EPA Web site at http://www.epa.gov.

noise levels of factories, highways, airports, and other locations. Some test noise levels of construction equipment, chain saws, lawn mowers, or other equipment. High noise levels can harm workers or the public.

Education and Training

Pollution control is highly technical work, so you should take as many mathematics (algebra and geometry) and laboratory science (chemistry, physics, and biology) courses as you can. Communications, computers, conservation, and ecology studies are also important.

After high school, you need to complete a two-year program in pollution control technology. These programs are offered at community and junior colleges, and at technical schools. Some employers also offer on-the-job training for new employees.

Earnings

Government entry-level salaries for pollution control technicians are about $16,400 to $20,600 per year, depending on education and experience. The average is $30,300 a year. Technicians who become managers or supervisors can make up to $50,000 a year or more.

Outlook

Demand for pollution control technicians should continue at an average pace through 2008. Those trained to handle complex technical demands will find the best jobs. All science technicians (including medical science, agricultural, and pollution control technicians) held about 227,000 jobs in 1998, according to the U.S. Department of Labor. The demand for pollution control technicians should continue due to public concern for the environment.

There will be jobs available wherever there is heavy industry and strict state and local pollution control laws. As long as the federal government supports pollution control, the pollution control industry will continue to grow.

FOR MORE INFO

The following organizations' members work in air pollution control, hazardous waste management, and groundwater quality control:

Air and Waste Management Association
One Gateway Center, Third Floor
Pittsburgh, PA 15222
412-232-3444
http://www.awma.org

Association of Groundwater Scientists and Engineers
6375 Riverside Drive
Dublin, OH 43017

U.S. Environmental Protection Agency
401 M Street, SW
Washington, DC 20460
202-260-2090
http://www.epa.gov

Water Environment Federation
601 Wythe Street
Alexandria, VA 22314-1994
703-684-2452
http://www.wef.org

Range Managers

BLM Facts

The Bureau of Land Management (BLM) manages 264 million acres of land—about one-eighth of the land in the United States—and about 300 million additional acres of subsurface mineral resources.

The BLM is responsible for wildfire management and suppression on 388 million acres.

Most of the lands the BLM manages are located in the western United States, including Alaska. They are dominated by extensive grasslands, forests, high mountains, arctic tundra, and deserts.

The BLM manages a wide variety of resources and uses, including energy and minerals; timber; forage; wild horse and burro populations; fish and wildlife habitat; wilderness areas; archaeological, paleontological, and historical sites; and other natural heritage values.

What Range Managers Do

Range managers help protect the environment, and improve and increase the food supply on ranges, which cover more than 1 billion acres of land in the western United States and in Alaska. Range managers also may be called *range scientists, range ecologists,* and *range conservationists.*

Ranges are the source of food for both livestock and wildlife, but overgrazing by animals can leave the land bare. When there is neither grass nor shrubs on open land, soil erosion occurs. Range managers are in charge of erosion-control programs, such as irrigation and rotating grazing lands.

Range managers make sure the land provides as rich a source of food as possible. They study rangelands to decide the number and kinds of cattle that can best graze on these lands and the times of year that are best for grazing. They also study different varieties of plants to deter-

A range manager discusses land renewal with a farmer.

mine which ones will grow best and which might actually be harmful to the land and its wildlife.

Range managers try to conserve the land for a variety of other uses, such as outdoor recreation, timber, and habitats for many kinds of wildlife. They look for ways to prevent damage by fire and rodents. If a fire does occur, range managers try to restore the land. They make sure fences and corrals are in good condition, and water reservoirs are well maintained.

Most range managers work in the western part of the United States or in Alaska, where most of the nation's rangelands are

EXPLORING

• Apply for a summer job on a ranch or a farm.

• Attend lectures given by range managers, ranchers, or conservation experts.

• Volunteer to work with conservation organizations.

NATURE **63**

STUDY SUBJECTS

Here are some courses that college students might take to prepare for a range-management career.

Rangeland Plant Communities focuses on the vegetation of western U.S. rangeland, identifying plant species, and human influence on plant communities.

Grazing Ecology and Management covers animal diet and nutrition, grazing behavior, and the interaction of vegetation, soil, and grazing animals; how to improve livestock production, protect wildlife habitat, protect watershed, and reproduce forests.

Range and Forest Management covers principles and technical procedures associated with management of rangeland and forest plant communities, including chemical, biological, and cultural treatments.

Rangeland Inventory and Monitoring covers techniques of mapping and measuring vegetation and soils for inventory and monitoring of rangelands.

Rangeland Management Plan Design teaches students how to conduct a field inventory, develop management alternatives, and write proposals for management plans.

---

located. Most range managers work for the federal government in the Forest Service, the Soil Conservation Service of the Department of Agriculture, the Bureau of Indian Affairs, or the Bureau of Land Management of the Department of the Interior. Other employers include state governments and oil and coal companies, which need experts to help repair the land damaged by mining and exploring for oil.

Education and Training

To prepare for a career as a range manager, take classes in biology, chemistry, physics, and mathematics. Business classes also will be helpful for learning aspects of management. Range managers must have a bachelor's degree in range science, soil science, or natural resource management. For many range manager positions you need a graduate degree in one of these fields.

Earnings

According to the U.S. Department of Labor, beginning range managers with bachelor's degrees working for the federal government earned between $20,600 and $25,500 in 1999. Those with master's degrees started between $25,500 and $31,200, and those with doctorates started at $37,700 or more. The average salary for all range managers was $46,300 in 1999. State governments and private companies pay their range managers salaries that are about the same as those paid by the federal government.

Outlook

Job growth for range managers will be about the same as the average for all occupations in the next decade. The growing demand for wildlife habitats, recreation, and water, and an increasing concern for the environment should create a need for range managers. A greater number of large ranches will employ range managers to improve range management practices and increase profits. Range specialists will also find jobs in private industry, reclaiming lands damaged by oil and coal exploration.

For More Info

Society for Range Management
445 Union Boulevard, Suite 230
Lakewood, CO 80228
303-986-3309
http://www.srm.org

U.S. Department of Agriculture
Natural Resources Conservation Service
14th and Independence Avenue
Washington, DC 20250
http://www.nrcs.usda.gov

U.S. Department of Agriculture
U.S. Forest Service
PO Box 96090
Washington, DC 20090-6090
http://www.fs.fed.us

U.S. Department of the Interior
Bureau of Land Management
1849 C Street, NW, Room 406-LS
Washington, DC 20240
202-452-5125
http://www.blm.gov/nhp

Soil Conservation Technicians

The Dirt on Soil

Soil is a combination of plant, animal, mineral, and other matter. It contains sand, silt, and clay particles, as well as water, air, and many different microorganisms.

Soil provides all but three of the 16 nutrients that plants need to grow. Soil also releases these nutrients into streams and oceans, where fish and other water life benefit from them.

Soil cleans water. Nearly all fresh water travels over soil or through soil before it enters rivers, lakes, and aquifers. The processes that take place in the upper layers of soil help remove many impurities from the water and kill some disease-causing organisms. Soil helps prevent flooding by soaking up large amounts of rain and distributing it to water bodies over days, months, or years.

Source: Soil and Water Conservation Society

What Soil Conservation Technicians Do

Soil conservation technicians help land users develop plans to use the soil wisely. They show farmers how to rotate their crops so that the nutrients in the soil are not exhausted. They also help foresters plan growth and harvesting cycles so that trees are not cut down before they mature.

Soil conservation technicians mainly work with farmers and agricultural concerns. They also work with land developers and local governments to prevent soil erosion and preserve wetlands.

Soil conservation technicians survey land, take soil samples, and help landowners select, install, and maintain measures that conserve and improve soil, plant, water, marsh, wildlife, and recreational resources. These measures might include contour cultivation, grass waterways, terracing, tree planting, field wind-

Consolidation Coal Company

A soil conservation technician studies the health of a wheat crop growing in soil that was once mined for coal.

breaks, irrigation ditches, grass seeding, and farm drains. Other practices for soil conservation are strip cropping, tillage practices, fertilization, pesticide application, and land leveling.

Soil technicians meet with landowners to help them decide on new conservation measures or modify existing ones. They might discuss new techniques and equipment or changes in soil fertility, pesticides, and herbicides. When a soil conservationist designs a new conservation plan for a landowner, technicians inspect the different phases of the project as it is constructed. They might inspect ponds, structures, dams, tile, outlet terraces, and animal waste control facilities.

EXPLORING

- Join a chapter of the 4-H Club or National FFA Organization.
- Visit these Web sites to learn more about soil conservation:
The Field Museum Underground Adventure
http://www.fmnh.org/ua/default.htm
The Pedosphere and Its Dynamics
http://www.pedosphere.com
Soil Science Education Home Page
http://ltpwww.gsfc.nasa.gov/globe/index.htm

Education and Training

Soil conservation technicians need a high school diploma. Courses in mathematics, speech, writing, chemistry, and biology are important. Courses in vocational agriculture, which is the study of farming as an occupation, are also helpful.

Some technical institutes and junior or community colleges offer associate's degrees in soil conservation. First-year courses in these programs include basic soils, chemistry, botany, zoology, and range management. Second-year courses include surveying, forestry, game management, fish management, and soil and water conservation.

Earnings

In 1999, the average annual salary for soil conservationists employed by the federal government was $48,900, according to the U.S. Department of Labor. Starting salaries ranged

NRCS AND CCC TO THE RESCUE

After the Dust Bowl, Congress established the Natural Resource Conservation Service (NRCS) of the U.S. Department of Agriculture in 1935. The job of reclaiming the land through wise conservation practices was not an easy one because more than 800 million tons of topsoil had already been blown away by the winds over the plains. In addition to the large areas of the Midwest which had become desert land, there were other badly eroded lands throughout the country.

The Civilian Conservation Corps (CCC) was created to help relieve unemployment during the Great Depression of the 1930s. It established camps in rural areas and assigned people to aid in many different kinds of conservation. Soil conservationists directed those portions of the CCC program designed to halt the loss of topsoil by wind and water action.

from $20,600 to $25,500 depending on academic achievement. Those with master's degrees earned higher starting salaries ranging from $25,500 to $31,200. Soil conservationists with doctorates start at $37,700 a year.

The salaries of conservationists and technicians working for private firms or agencies are about the same as those paid by the federal government. Earnings at the state and local levels are usually lower.

Outlook

Employment is expected to grow about as fast as the average in this field. Most soil conservationists and technicians are employed by the federal government, so employment opportunities will depend in large part on government spending. Most of America's cropland has suffered from some sort of erosion, so soil conservation professionals will be needed to help prevent a dangerous depletion of fertile soil.

For More Info

American Society of Agronomy
Career Development and
Placement Service
677 South Segoe Road
Madison, WI 53711
608-273-8080
headquarters@agronomy.org
http://www.agronomy.org

Soil and Water Conservation Society
7515 Northeast Ankeny Road
Ankeny, IA 50021
515-289-2331
http://www.swcs.org

Natural Resources Conservation Service
U.S. Department of Agriculture
Attn: Conservation Communications Staff
PO Box 2890
Washington, DC 20013
http://www.nrcs.usda.gov

Related Jobs

Agricultural Scientists
Farm Crop Production Technicians
Foresters
Geologists
Groundwater Professionals
Meteorologists
Range Managers
Soil Scientists
Surveyors

Soil Scientists

Dirty Artwork

The appeal of soil study isn't always scientific; sometimes the beauty of the soil inspires scientists. Hungarian soil scientist Erika Micheli discovered a collection of wavy, multicolored soil layers after a surface mining operation left the ground exposed. The rippled formations were made by the burrowing of prehistoric groundhogs, erosion, and pressure from frozen rainwater. Micheli's study of the formations led to cautions to area farmers about the way they used fertilizers and pesticides.

The formations also inspired Micheli to create works of art in the form of lacquered, 3-D portraits of the soil.

What Soil Scientists Do

Soil is one of our most important natural resources. It provides the nutrients necessary to grow food for hundreds of millions of people. To use soil wisely and keep it from washing away or being damaged, experts must analyze it and find the best ways to manage it. *Soil scientists* are these experts. Soil scientists collect soil samples and study their chemical and physical characteristics. They study how soil responds to fertilizers and other farming practices. This helps farmers decide what types of crops to grow on certain soils.

Soil scientists do much of their work outdoors. They go to fields to take soil samples. They spend many hours meeting with farmers and discussing ways to avoid soil damage. They may suggest that a farmer grow crops on different parts of a farm every few years so that the unused soil can recover. Soil scientists may also recommend that a farmer use various fertilizers to put nutrients back into the soil.

A soil scientist tests ground water levels to see if there is enough water to support plant life.

They may suggest ways to cover crops to keep the wind from blowing the soil away.

Soil scientists work for agricultural research laboratories, crop production companies, and other organizations. They also work with road departments to advise them about the quality and condition of the soil over which roads will be built.

Some soil scientists travel to foreign countries to conduct research and

EXPLORING

• If you live in an agricultural community, look for part-time or summer work on a farm or ranch.

• A local 4-H club or FFA program can teach you about farming and agriculture.

observe the way other scientists treat the soil. Many also teach at colleges, universities, and agricultural schools.

Education and Training

To be a soil scientist, you need a solid background in mathematics and science, especially the physical and earth sciences. You should also be curious, be able to solve complex problems, and have good writing and speaking skills.

The best way to become a soil scientist is to go to college and earn a bachelor's degree. Then you should go on to earn a master's degree in agricultural science. A degree in biology, physics, or chemistry might also be enough, but you should take some courses in agriculture. With a bachelor's degree in agricultural science, you can get some nonresearch jobs, but you will not be able to advance very far. Most research and teaching positions require a doctorate.

WORDS TO LEARN

Aeration porosity: The fraction of the volume of soil that is filled with air at any given time.

Blowout: A small area from which soil material has been removed by wind.

Creep: Slow mass movement of soil and soil material down steep slopes primarily under the influence of gravity, but aided by saturation with water and by alternate freezing and thawing.

Dunes: Wind-built ridges and hills of sand formed in the same manner as snowdrifts.

Gytta: Peat consisting of plant and animal residues from standing water.

Karst: Topography with caves, sinkholes, and underground drainage that is formed in limestone and other rocks by dissolution.

Macronutrient: A nutrient found in high concentrations in a plant.

Scarp: A cliff or steep slope along the margin of a plateau.

Earnings

In 1999, agricultural scientists earned from $24,200 to $79,800, with a median of $42,300 a year, according to the U.S. Department of Labor. Soil scientists in government jobs earn average yearly salaries of about $53,000. Those with Ph.D.s earned $67,000 to $87,000 a year. Soil scientists in private industry earn about the same salaries.

Outlook

Agricultural problems will continue to be important in the coming years. Soil scientists should find plenty of job opportunities. There have not been as many agricultural students in the past few years as there were in the past, so schools will probably be optimistic about accepting new students and placing new graduates in jobs.

Soil scientists will be able to find jobs with private companies, such as seed, fertilizer, and farm equipment companies, as well as with government agencies. There will be more opportunities in teaching and in research.

FOR MORE INFO

To learn about careers and issues that affect soil scientists, contact these organizations:

American Society of Agronomy
677 South Segoe Road
Madison, WI 53711
608-273-8080
http://www.agronomy.org

National Society of Consulting Soil Scientists
325 Pennsylvania Avenue SE, Suite 700
Washington, DC 20003
800-535-7148
http://www.nscss.org

For a career resources booklet, contact:
Soil Science Society of America
677 South Segoe Road
Madison, WI 53711
608-273-8095
http://www.soils.org

Tree Experts

Signs of Danger

There are clues that tell you when a tree might pose a danger to your safety. Look for these signs:

Large branches attached with tight, V-shaped forks

Cracks in the trunk or major limbs

Hollow or decayed areas

A lot of dead wood

Mushrooms growing from the base of the tree or under its canopy

Branches close to electric power lines

What Tree Experts Do

Tree experts, sometimes called *arborists,* practice arboriculture, which is the care of trees and shrubs, especially those in urban areas. Trees and shrubs need more than just sunlight and water to survive. They also need routine care, occasional diagnosis, and treatment.

Tree experts prune trees to control their shape. They trim branches if they interfere with power lines, cross property lines, or grow too close to buildings. Tree experts use pruning shears, or hand and power saws to do the cutting. If the branches are large or cumbersome, tree experts may rope them together before they begin to saw. After they are cut, the branches can be safely lowered to the ground. Ladders, aerial lifts, and cranes help tree experts reach extremely tall trees. Sometimes, cables or braces are used on tree limbs weakened by disease or old age, or damaged by a storm.

When cities or towns plan a new development they consult with tree experts to determine what types of trees to plant. Tree experts suggest the best trees for a particular environment.

A large part of keeping a tree healthy is the prevention of disease. There are a number of diseases, insects, bacteria, fungi, viruses, and other organisms that can be fatal to trees. Tree experts are trained to diagnose the problem and suggest the proper remedy. For example, they might recommend chemical insecticides or the use of natural insect predators to combat an insect problem.

Trees, especially young plantings, often need extra nourishment. Tree experts are trained to apply fertilizers, both natural and chemical, in a safe and environmentally friendly manner. They are also hired by golf courses and parks to install lightning protection systems for trees.

Education and Training

Biology classes can provide a solid background for a career in arboriculture. An interest in gardening, conservation, or the outdoors is also helpful. Entry-level positions such as assistants or climbers do not require advanced education. If you

EXPLORING

Here are some tree resources to explore:

First Guide to Trees (Peterson Field Guides) by George A. Petrides and Roger Tory Peterson (Houghton Miflin, 1998).

Trees: Trees Identified by Leaf, Bark & Seed by Steven M. L. Aronson (Workman Publishing Group, 1998).

International Arboriculture Trees and Timber
http://www.arborists.com

The World of Trees
http://www.domtar.com/arbre/english

TreeGuide
http://www.treeguide.com

plan to make this field your career, a college education will help you advance to higher positions and earn a better salary. Several colleges and universities offer arboriculture and related programs, such as landscape design, nursery stock production, or grounds and turf maintenance.

On-the-job instruction lasting about one to three months is available for some positions. Trainees get their start by loading and unloading the equipment, gathering debris, and assisting other workers. In time, trainees are allowed to operate small pieces of equipment. After sufficient observation and experience, workers are allowed to climb trees and operate larger pieces of machinery.

Earnings

Entry-level positions, such as grounds workers or trainees,

SACRIFICING LIMBS FOR SAFETY

Homeowners can get upset when a trimming crew shows up to prune the trees on their property. But trees can cause property damage and power outages that are expensive and dangerous. According to the National Arborist Association, tree failure is the leading cause of power outages nationwide.

Utility companies have to make sure power lines are safe, so they specify the amount of clearance that must be maintained around wires. These companies are also required to follow care standards to keep trees healthy and beautiful. It is better for the tree if the trimmers remove whole limbs using a small number of large cuts, than if they make numerous small cuts and leave stubbed branches. Sometimes utility-company trimmers remove entire limbs to help train future growth of the tree away from wires. These measures, which may seem drastic to homeowners, are important for the safety of trees and people.

pay between $7 and $10 an hour. Supervisors with three or more years of experience earn from $20 to $30 an hour. Private consultants with eight to 10 years of experience or arborists in sales positions can earn $50,000 to $60,000 or more annually. Arborists servicing busy urban areas tend to earn more.

Outlook

The outlook for careers in arboriculture is promising. The public's increasing interest in the planning and the preservation of the environment has increased demand for tree experts. A healthy economy is another factor. According to Gallup's 1999 U.S. Homeowner Landscaping, Lawn Care, and Tree Care Survey, 24 million homeowners in the United States spent approximately $17.4 billion on professional landscape and care.

For More Info

To find out more about a career as an arborist, contact:
National Tree Experts Association
PO Box 1094
Amherst, NH 03031-1094
603-673-3311
http://www.natlarb.com

For industry and career information, or to receive a copy of Arborist News *or* Careers in Aboriculture, *contact:*
International Society of Arboriculture
PO 3129
Champaign, IL 61826-3129
217-355-9411
isa@isa-arbor.com
http://www.ag.uiuc.edu/~isa

For industry and career information, a listing of practicing arborists, or educational programs at the university level, contact:
National Arborists Association, Inc.
3 Perimeter Road, Unit 1
Manchester, NH 03103
603-314-5380
NAA@natlarb.com
http://www.natlarb.com

For industry information, membership requirements, or for a copy of City Trees, *contact:*
Society of Municipal Arborists
PO Box 11521
St. Louis, MO 63105
314-862-3325
http://www.urban-forestry.com

Wildlife Photographers

Photo Galleries on the Web

These Web sites all have photo galleries, as well as lots of information about wildlife, habitat conservation, and endangered species.

U.S. Fish and Wildlife Service
http://www.fws.gov

National Wildlife Federation
http://www.nwf.org/nwf

World Wildlife Fund
http://www.worldwildlife.org

Zooweb: How to Take Great Pictures at the Zoo
http://www.zooweb.net/photos.htm

What Wildlife Photographers Do

Wildlife photographers take photographs and make films of animals in their natural environment. Wildlife photographers provide the photographs for science publications, research reports, textbooks, newspapers, magazines, and many other printed materials. Films are used in research and for professional and public education.

Wildlife photographers often find themselves in swamps, deserts, jungles, at the tops of trees or in underground tunnels, swimming in the ocean or hanging from the side of a mountain. They may shoot pictures of the tiniest insects or the largest mammals.

Some wildlife photographers specialize in one family or species or in one region or area. For example, some wildlife photographers may shoot chimpanzees in their various habitats around the world. Another photographer might shoot various species of birds that live in the southwestern United States.

Like other professional photographers, wildlife photographers must know about light, camera settings, lenses, film, and filters. In addition, they must be able to take pictures without disturbing the animals or natural settings that they photograph. To do this, they must research the animals and plants they use as subjects before they go into the wild.

Wildlife photographers do not necessarily need to be zoologists, although a background in biology or zoology is helpful for this career. After many years of experience, wildlife photographers often become experts in the behavior of the animals they photograph. It is also possible for zoologists who use photography in their research to eventually become expert wildlife photographers.

The technological advances in photographic equipment and the expertise of wildlife photographers have contributed much to scientific knowledge about animal behavior, new species, evolution, and animals' roles in preserving or changing the environment.

EXPLORING

• Take classes in photography, media arts (film, sound recording), and life sciences.

• Join photography clubs or enter contests that encourage you to use camera equipment.

• Learn how to use different types of film, lenses, and filters.

• Practice taking pictures of birds and animals at parks, nature centers, and zoos.

• Watch nature shows and videos to learn more about both animal behavior and filming animals in the wild.

BE A PRO: TIPS FOR TAKING WILDLIFE PHOTOS

- Study the animals you want to photograph before you go out. Learn about their eating, sleeping, and other behaviors so you will know what to expect.

- Plan ahead and take the right kind and amount of film you need. Consider the light and weather conditions. Take extra camera batteries.

- Wear dark clothes that blend in with surroundings.

- Don't stand where you will stick out like a sore thumb. Stay in shadows near trees or shrubs.

- Keep your distance.

- Be patient and alert. While you are waiting to take a photo or shoot film of a particular animal, you may see dozens of other opportunities to shoot other birds, insects, and animals around you.

Education and Training

There are no formal education requirements for becoming a wildlife photographer. A high school diploma is recommended for this career, and earning a college degree will help you learn about both photography and biology. A bachelor of arts in photography or film with a minor in biology would prepare you well for a career as a wildlife photographer. During your education, you should try to gain practical experience and build a portfolio of your work.

Wildlife photographers must not risk the well-being of any animal to take a picture. They must show concern for the environment in their work. They must use common sense and not anger or frighten any animals while trying to take a picture.

Earnings

Full-time wildlife photographers earn average salaries of about $25,000 to $38,000 a year. Most wildlife photographers work as freelancers. Wildlife photographers who combine scientific training and photographic expertise usually start at higher salaries than other photographers. It can be difficult to earn a living as a wildlife photographer, so you may have to supplement your income with another occupation or do other kinds of photography until you earn a reputation.

Outlook

Employment of photographers will increase more slowly than the average through 2008. The demand for new photographs and videos of animals in their natural habitats should remain strong in research, education, communication, and entertainment.

For More Info

American Film Institute
2021 North Western Avenue
Los Angeles, CA 90027
323-856-7600
info@afionline.org
http://www.afionline.org

Professional Photographers of America
229 Peachtree Street, NE, No. 2200
Atlanta, GA 30303-2206
800-786-6277
membership@ppa.world.org
http://www.ppa.com

Wildlife Research Photography
PO Box 3628
Mammoth Lakes, CA 93546-3628
760-924-8632
http://www.moose395.net

Related Jobs

Biologists
Cinematographers
Film Directors and Producers
Naturalists
Photographers
Zoologists

Zoologists

Hope for the Manatees

Surveys show that there are no more than 700 West Indian manatees left in their habitat off the coast of Belize in Central America. There may be as few as 300. They have been killed or injured by boats or harmed by pollution from inland activities and deforestation. They have even been killed and marketed as fish (even though they are mammals).

A research program started by the Wildlife Preservation Trust International may offer hope to the endangered manatee. The environmental air force called LightHawk is charting the manatee's range and behavior. The data collected will be used to plan ways to save the manatee from extinction.

What Zoologists Do

Zoologists are biologists who study animals. They usually specialize in one animal group. *Entomologists* are experts on insects. *Ornithologists* study birds. *Mammalogists* focus on mammals. *Herpetologists* specialize in reptiles. *Ichthyologists* study fish. Some zoologists specialize even more and focus on a specific part or aspect of an animal. For example, a zoologist might study single-celled organisms, a particular variety of fish, or the behavior of one group of animals, such as elephants or bees.

Some zoologists are primarily teachers. Others spend most of their time doing research. Nearly all zoologists spend a major portion of their time at the computer. Most zoologists spend very little time outdoors (an average of two to eight weeks per year). In fact, junior scientists often spend more time in the field than senior scientists do. Senior scientists coordinate research, supervise other

82 DISCOVERING CAREERS FOR YOUR FUTURE

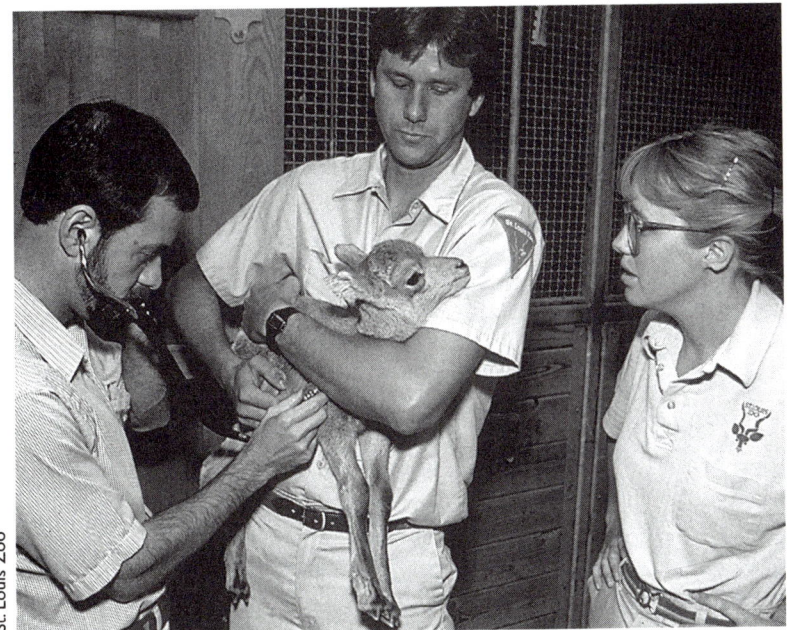

A mammalogist at a nature preserve does a routine check on one of the preserve's animals as part of an ongoing research study.

workers, and try to find funding. Raising money is an extremely important activity for zoologists who work for government agencies or universities.

Basic research zoologists conduct experiments on live or dead animals, in a laboratory or in natural surroundings. They make discoveries that might help humans. Such research in the past has led to discoveries about nutrition, aging, food production, and pest control. Some research zoologists work in the field with wild animals, such as whales. They trace their movements with radio transmitters and observe their eating habits, mating patterns, and other behavior. Researchers use all kinds of laboratory chemicals and equipment such as dissecting tools,

EXPLORING

• Volunteer at your local zoo or aquarium.

• Ask your school librarian to help you find books and videos on animal behavior.

• Explore hobbies such as birdwatching, insect collecting, or raising hamsters, rabbits, and other pets.

• Offer to pet sit for your neighbors. This will give you a chance to observe and care for animals.

ANIMAL FUN FACTS

- The world's largest dog on record was an Old English Mastiff, named Zorba. In 1989, Zorba weighed 343 pounds and was 8 feet 3 inches long from nose to tail.
- The smallest dog on record was a Yorkie from Blackburn, England, who was 2.5 inches tall and 3.75 inches long. He weighed only 4 ounces.
- The world's smallest cat on record is a male Blue Point Himalayan-Persian named Tinker Toy. He is 2.75 inches tall and 7.5 inches long.
- The largest feline on record is a Siberian tiger named Jaipur. Jaipur is 10 feet 11 inches long and weighs 932 pounds. He lives in New Jersey.
- The cheetah is the fastest land animal. It is the only cat that can't retract its claws.
- The world's largest bird is the male African ostrich. They have been recorded to measure 9 feet tall and weigh 345 pounds.
- The world's smallest bird is the adult male bee hummingbird of Cuba. It is 2.24 inches long and weighs 0.056 ounces.

Source: Amazing Animal Facts at http://zebu.cvm.msu.edu/~dawsonbr/

microscopes, slides, electron microscopes, and other sophisticated machinery.

Zoologists in applied research use basic research to solve problems in medicine, conservation, and aquarium and zoo work. For example, applied researchers may develop a new drug for people or animals, a new pesticide, or a new type of pet food.

Many zoologists teach in colleges and universities while they do their own research. Some zoologists manage zoos and aquariums. Still others work for government agencies, private businesses, and research organizations.

Education and Training

Science classes, especially in biology, are important if you want to become a zoologist. You should also study English, communications, and computer science.

After high school, you must go to college to earn a bachelor's degree. A master's or doctoral degree is usually also required. You do not need to specialize until you enter a master's degree program.

Earnings

Beginning salaries in private industry average $29,000 a year for zoologists with bachelor's degrees in biological science. Those with master's degrees earn $34,000 a year. Zoologists with doctoral degrees earn about $46,000 a year. General biological scientists who work for the federal government earn average salaries of about $48,600.

FOR MORE INFO

For information about all areas of zoology, contact:
Society for Integrative and Comparative Biology
1313 Dolley Madison Boulevard, Suite 402
McLean, VA 22201
800-955-1236
http://www.sicb.org

For information about zoological activities and organizations, schools, internships, and job opportunities, contact:
American Institute of Biological Sciences
1444 Eye Street, NW, Suite 200
Washington, DC 20005
202-628-1500
http://www.aibs.org

Outlook

Although job growth in the field of zoology has been slow in recent years, that should change in the next few years. This is because there is more interest in preserving the environment. There will be a lot of competition for research jobs.

Glossary

accredited: Approved as meeting established standards for providing good training and education. This approval is usually given by an independent organization of professionals to a school or a program in a school. Compare **certified** and **licensed**.

apprentice: A person who is learning a trade by working under the supervision of a skilled worker. Apprentices often receive classroom instruction in addition to their supervised practical experience.

apprenticeship: 1. A program for training apprentices (see apprentice). 2. The period of time when a person is an apprentice. In highly skilled trades, apprenticeships may last three or four years.

associate's degree: An academic rank or title granted by a community or junior college or similar institution to graduates of a two-year program of education beyond high school.

bachelor's degree: An academic rank or title given to a person who has completed a four-year program of study at a college or university. Also called an undergraduate degree or baccalaureate.

certified: Approved as meeting established requirements for skill, knowledge, and experience in a particular field. People are certified by the organization of professionals in their field. Compare **accredited** and **licensed**.

community college: A public two-year college, attended by students who do not live at the college. Graduates of a community college receive an associate degree and may transfer to a four-year college or university to complete a bachelor's degree. Compare **junior college** and **technical college**.

diploma: A certificate or document given by a school to show that a person has completed a course or has graduated from the school.

doctorate: An academic rank or title (the highest) granted by a graduate school to a person who has completed a two- to three-year program after having received a master's degree.

fringe benefit: A payment or benefit to an employee in addition to regular wages or salary. Examples of fringe benefits include a pension, a paid vacation, and health or life insurance.

graduate school: A school that people may attend after they have received their bachelor's degree. People who complete an educational program at a graduate school earn a master's degree or a doctorate.

intern: An advanced student (usually one with at least some college training) in a professional field who is employed in a job that is intended to provide supervised practical experience for the student.

internship: 1. The position or job of an intern (see intern). 2. The period of time when a person is an intern.

junior college: A two-year college that offers courses like those in the first half of a four-year college program. Graduates of a junior college usually receive an associate degree and may transfer to a four-year college or university to complete a bachelor's degree. Compare **community college.**

liberal arts: The subjects covered by college courses that develop broad general knowledge rather than specific occupational skills. The liberal arts are often considered to include philosophy, literature and the arts, history, language, and some courses in the social sciences and natural sciences.

licensed: Having formal permission from the proper authority to carry out an activity that would be illegal without that permission. For example, a person may be licensed to practice medicine or to drive a car. Compare **certified**.

major: (in college) The academic field in which a student specializes and receives a degree.

master's degree: An academic rank or title granted by a graduate school to a person who has completed a one- or two-year program after having received a bachelor's degree.

pension: An amount of money paid regularly by an employer to a former employee after he or she retires from working.

private: 1. Not owned or controlled by the government (such as private industry or a private employment agency). 2. Intended only for a particular person or group; not open to all (such as a private road or a private club).

public: 1. Provided or operated by the government (such as a public library). 2. Open and available to everyone (such as a public meeting).

regulatory: Having to do with the rules and laws for carrying out an activity. A regulatory agency, for example, is a government organization that sets up required procedures for how certain things should be done.

scholarship: A gift of money to a student to help the student pay for further education.

social studies: Courses of study (such as civics, geography, and history) that deal with how human societies work.

starting salary: Salary paid to a newly hired employee. The starting salary is usually a smaller amount than is paid to a more experienced worker.

technical college: A private or public college offering two- or four-year programs in technical subjects. Technical colleges offer courses in both general and technical subjects and award associate degrees and bachelor's degrees.

technician: A worker with specialized practical training in a mechanical or scientific subject who works under the supervision of scientists, engineers, or other professionals. Technicians typically receive two years of college-level education after high school.

technologist: A worker in a mechanical or scientific field with more training than a technician. Technologists typically must have between two and four years of college-level education after high school.

undergraduate: A student at a college or university who has not yet received a degree.

undergraduate degree: See **bachelor's degree**.

union: An organization whose members are workers in a particular industry or company. The union works to gain better wages, benefits, and working conditions for its members. Also called a labor union or trade union.

vocational school: A public or private school that offers training in one or more skills or trades. Compare **technical college**.

wage: Money that is paid in return for work done, especially money paid on the basis of the number of hours or days worked.

Index of Job Titles

adventure travel specialists, **6-9**
agricultural scientists, 73
aquatic biologists, 10
arborists, **74-77**

basic research zoologists, 83
biological oceanographers, 52
biological scientists, 10, 85
biologists, **10-13**, 26, 82
botanists, 10, **14-17**

chemists, 10
conservation professionals, 45
conservation scientists, 32
conservationists, 47
criminal investigators, 27

ecologists, 15, **18-21**, 46
engineers, 26
entomologists, 82
environmental educators, 46
environmental engineers, **22-25**
environmental protection specialists, 25
environmental technicians, 58
environmental workers, 21
ethnobotanists, 15

farmers, 19, 70
fish and game wardens, **26-29**
fish and wildlife wardens, 47
forest ecologists, 16, 18, 31

forest engineers, 31
foresters, **30-33**

geochemical oceanographers, 52
geological oceanographers, 52
geological technicians, 36
geologists, 10, **34-37**
geophysical oceanographers, 53
grounds workers, 76
guides, 7, 9

hazardous waste management technicians, **38-41**
hazardous waste technicians, **38-41**
herpetologists, 82
horticultural technicians, 16

ichthyologists, 82
inspectors and compliance officers, 25

land trust managers, **42-45**
land trust or preserve managers, **42-45**
law enforcement agents, 26
life scientists, 10

mammalogists, 82
marine biologists, 52
marine geologists, 34

microbiologists, 12, 13
mycologists, 16

naturalists, **46-49**
nature resource managers, 46

oceanographers, **50-53**
ornithologists, 82
outfitters, 7

paleontologists, 34
park rangers, **54-57**
petroleum geologists, 34
physical oceanographers, 52
physicists, 10
plant cytologists, 16
plant geneticists, 16
pollution control technicians, **58-61**
population ecologists, 19
preserve managers, 42-45

range conservationists, 62
range ecologists, 62
range managers, 32, 47, **62-65**
range scientists, 62

rangers, 54, 55, 57
realty specialists, 26
refuge managers, 27
refuge officers, 26
refuge rangers, 26, 27
research botanists, 15

science technicians, 41
silviculturists, 31
soil conservation technicians, **66-69**
soil conservationists, 32, 67-69
soil scientists, **70-73**
soil technicians, 66-69
special agents, 27, 29

travel agents, 9
tree experts, **74-77**

wildlife conservationists, 26, 46
wildlife inspectors, 26, 27
wildlife managers, 26, 47
wildlife photographers, **78-81**

zoologists, 10, 79, **82-85**

Nature on the Web

Backyard Conservation
http://fb-net.org/backyard.htm

BBC Online Nature Homepage
http://www.bbc.co.uk/nature

Biodiversity
http://www.worldwildlife.org/windows/ecoregion

Environmental Issues
http://environment.about.com/mbody.htm

Environmental Protection Agency
http://www.epa.gov

National Park Service NatureNet
http://www.nature.nps.gov/

The Nature Conservancy
http://www.nature.org

World Wildlife Fund
http://www.worldwildlife.org